CAVES OF HOPE

CAVES OF HOPE

Story of Nuba Faith, Resilience and Liberation

Archbishop Dr. Paul Benjamin Yugusuk (Pawolo)

Ekklesia Society Publication

Copyright © 2026 Archbishop Dr. Paul Benjamin Yugusuk (Pawolo)

All rights reserved.

ISBN 978-0-9913533-5-4

No part of this publication may be reproduced, stored in a retrieval system, or transmitted in any form or by any means—electronic, mechanical, photocopying, recording, or otherwise—without the prior written permission of the author, except for brief quotations used in reviews, scholarly articles, or pastoral teaching with proper attribution.

This book is a testimony of faith, resilience, and liberation. It is offered as a gift to the Nuba people and all communities seeking peace, dignity, and spiritual renewal. Any use of its content must honor its purpose and the integrity of its witness.

Educational use is welcomed when it serves the mission of healing, unity, and biblical truth. Teachers, clergy, and students may reference this work in sermons, study guides, and theological reflection—provided that the author is credited and the message remains intact.

Published by
Ekklesia Society Publication
P. O Box 5343
Frisco, Texas 75035 USA 1.800.393.6267

For permissions, inquiries, or educational use:
Email: shalomsudan@yahoo.com official email
Phone: +211925620031/+254722980628

Dedication

To the indomitable spirit of the Nuba people — who turned caves into sanctuaries, suffering into strength, and silence into song.

You who prayed beneath the earth while bombs rained from the sky.
You who carried the wounded — with bare hands and unbroken hearts.
You who taught the world that faith is not fragile, and hope is not hollow.

Your courage defied the cruelty of war. Your resilience rewrote the story of survival.

Your dignity stood taller than the mountains that dared to shelter you.

This book is a tribute to your sacred endurance —
to the songs sung in darkness,
to the children born in hiding,
to the elders who refused to forget,
and to the generations who still rise,
with memory as their shield,
and liberation as their prayer

May your story echo across generations,
as a hymn of hope,
carved in stone and spirit

Acknowledgment

With deep reverence, I honor the enduring legacy of the Nuba clergy and liberators whose ministry and struggle among the Nuba people illuminated the darkest valleys with the light of Christ. Their lives were a living epistle—embodying the Gospel of peace, offering sanctuary to the afflicted, voice to the silenced, and healing to the brokenhearted. Their witness continues to inspire all who labor for justice, reconciliation, and hope amid suffering.

"Faith is taking the first step
even when you don't see the whole staircase."
– Martin Luther King Jr.

I extend my heartfelt gratitude to all who supported the development and publication of *Caves of Hope: Story of Nuba Faith, Resilience and Liberation.* Your encouragement, prayers, and partnership have been instrumental in bringing this work to fruition. May this volume serve not only as a scholarly contribution but also as a testament to the resilience of faith and the transformative power of communal solidarity.

-- Archbishop Dr. Paul Benjamin Yugusuk (Pawolo), Author
Caves of Hope: Story of Nuba Faith, Resilience and Liberation.

Contents

Foreword

With solemn awe and unwavering conviction, I present this sacred testimony from Archbishop Dr. Paul Benjamin Yugusuk (Pawolo). As Archbishop of Central Equatoria Internal Province in the Episcopal Church of South Sudan, he has served with steadfast faith, courageous compassion, and prophetic clarity—bringing light into some of the darkest corners of our region.

This book transcends the boundaries of a mission report. It is a sacred chronicle of divine encounter, communal endurance, and prophetic witness. It bears the cries of the Nuba people and the unmistakable presence of God, who walked with Archbishop Pawolo through war-torn mountains, bombed villages, and hidden caves where hope flickered like candlelight in the shadows.

I vividly recall the moment I assigned Archbishop Pawolo to the Nuba Mountains. It was a time of relentless bombardment and humanitarian crisis—when many feared to go, and few dared to stand with the people of Nuba. Yet Pawolo accepted the call with humility and boldness, embodying the servant heart of Christ. His mission was not only pastoral but profoundly prophetic: to be a living witness of God's love among a people under siege.

When he returned and shared his testimony at All Saints Cathedral in Juba, the cathedral became a sanctuary of shared lament and awakening. Tears flowed not only from sorrow, but from the recognition of God's enduring mercy. NGO representatives, Nuba intellectuals, and worshippers alike raised their hands in awe of God's faithfulness. The Spirit compelled its telling—not merely to honor the Nuba people, but to pierce the conscience of a world too long indifferent.

This book breaks the silence of decades. It documents the atrocities, the displacement, and the spiritual endurance of a people who have been marginalized and forgotten. Yet it also reveals the ripple effect of mercy, the power of small acts of kindness, and the hope that springs from faith in a God who liberates.

I commend Archbishop Pawolo for his obedience to God's call and for his courage to speak truth with love. This book is the fruit of that mission—a testimony born from the ashes of suffering and the light of divine presence. May it stir hearts, inspire action, and become a beacon of solidarity for all who seek justice and peace in South Sudan and beyond.

Let us journey with the Nuba people—in prayer, advocacy, and compassion—until justice rolls down like waters, and their faith shines like dawn breaking over the mountains.

-- Archbishop Dr. Daniel Deng Bul
Retired Primate of the Episcopal Church of South Sudan

Preface

In the heart of the Nuba Mountains, where silence speaks louder than words and suffering carves itself into stone, a people have not merely endured—they have believed, resisted, and risen.

Caves of Hope is not just a chronicle of hardship; it is a sacred witness to the faith that flourishes in the shadows, the resilience that defies despair, and the liberation that begins with a cry and ends in communion.

This book was born in the belly of the earth—in caves where prayers echoed against rock walls, where mothers whispered lullabies amid bombardment, and where the Word of God was preached with trembling hands and unwavering conviction. It is a testimony shaped by blood and baptism, by exile and embrace, by the Spirit's breath in the dust of affliction.

As Archbishop of Central Equatoria Internal Province, I have walked with the Nuba people through valleys of grief and mountaintops of grace. I have seen children sing among ruins, elders bless their enemies, and communities gather around scripture as if it were daily bread.

Caves of Hope is both a call to remember and a call to act. It invites church leaders, humanitarian partners, diaspora communities, and all people of conscience to bear witness—to see the Nuba not as victims, but as visionaries. Their caves are not tombs; they are wombs of transformation.

May this book stir your spirit, challenge your comfort, and awaken your courage. May it lead you to prayer, to partnership, and to prophetic solidarity. And may the Nuba story ripple across nations—until every cave becomes a cathedral of hope.

In Christ's mercy and mission,
Archbishop Dr. Paul Benjamin Yugusuk (Pawolo)
Juba, South Sudan, 2025

[

Introduction

This book is a living testimony—a flame of faith, resilience, and divine mercy kindled in the caves of Nuba. It chronicles my mission to the Nuba Mountains, a journey ignited by urgent cries and sealed by divine calling. Sent by the Episcopal Church of South Sudan and Sudan, I traveled to Nuba in response to reports of grave atrocities against innocent Nubian tribes.

What I encountered was a humanitarian crisis of staggering proportions: civilians wounded by airstrikes, hospitals overwhelmed, and entire communities displaced by violence. Yet amid the chaos, the unmistakable hand of God moved among us.

I navigated bomb-riddled terrain, delivered medical aid, and prayed with the suffering. From perilous landings to miraculous deliverance, every step of the journey bore witness to divine intervention. Where others saw despair, I saw hope. Where war carved scars, I witnessed healing. And in the eyes of the wounded, the displaced, and the faithful—I saw the face of Christ.

This book is not merely a report; it is a spiritual witness. It reveals how God protected me and the people of Nuba, how He provided medicine, comfort, and strength in the darkest hours. It is a summons to conscience: to see with compassion, to feel with conviction, and to respond with courage to the cries of those who have endured decades of oppression, marginalization, and silence.

The Nuba people remain hopeful. Their faith is unshaken. Their endurance is a living sermon. Their story must be told—not only to honor their suffering, but to inspire solidarity, advocacy, and healing.

In the caves where families hide from bombs, in the makeshift hospitals where nurses work without supplies, and in the broken villages where children still sing hymns of praise—I witnessed a nation preserved by the mercy of God.

Their resilience is not merely human; it is divine. Their survival is no accident—it is providence in motion, mercy incarnate.

As you read these pages, may your heart be stirred. May you see the face of Christ in the caves, the hospitals, and the broken villages. And may you join us in the mission to bring light, justice, and restoration to Nuba—a nation under God's preservation.

Let this book be a bridge—between suffering and compassion, silence and testimony, despair and hope. May it carry the light of Christ into every cave, every wound, and every heart that longs for healing.

Chapter One

The Genesis of Injustice: A Sacred Witness from the Nuba Mountains

Long before bombs shattered the skies and caves became sanctuaries, the suffering of the Nuba people had already begun. It traces back to 1956—the year Sudan gained independence. From that moment, seeds of marginalization, ethnic segregation, and land dispossession were sown.

The birth of a nation became, for the Nuba, the beginning of a long exile from justice.

Before the foundations of injustice were laid, the Nuba walked in covenant with the land. Their footsteps echoed harmony, their farming rhythms honored ancestry, and their hills bore witness to peace.

Betrayed Promises

Citizenship Denied, Identity Dismissed (1956–1967)

The promises of unity and freedom were written in the constitution but not in the hearts of those who governed. The Nuba, rich in culture and faith, were quickly branded as outsiders in their own land. Their languages were ignored, their customs were dismissed, and their presence was treated as an inconvenience to the new elite.

From the very beginning, the Nuba were not seen as citizens—they were managed as obstacles. But injustice does not remain static—it evolves. What began as exclusion soon took root in the soil itself.

Mechanized Farming and the Erosion of Harmony When Machines Replaced Memory (1968–1970)

In 1968, the government in Khartoum introduced mechanized farming across the fertile lands surrounding the Nuba Mountains. These large-scale agricultural schemes, designed to benefit elite investors, disrupted traditional land use and fractured the harmony between Arab tribes, such as the Baggara, and the indigenous Nuba people.

The soil, once shared in peace, became a battleground of greed.

The arrival of machines did not bring progress to the Nuba—it brought displacement. The ancestral farming rhythms, passed down through generations, were replaced by industrial schedules and foreign ownership. The land no longer responded to the footsteps of its caretakers; it was allocated, allocated again, and sold.

The covenant between soil and soul was broken.

The Baggara, once peaceful neighbors, found their grazing lands blocked by wealthy landowners who had seized the soil. In retaliation, they invaded ancestral Nuba lands and began to settle. The rhythm of coexistence was broken. Suspicion replaced trust.

The Nuba, caught between state-backed land grabs and tribal incursions, watched their sacred hills become contested zones. The elders who once mediated disputes with wisdom and prayer were silenced by bureaucrats and soldiers.

The land, once a covenant of peace, became a ledger of conquest.

Then came the Unregistered Land Act of 1970—a directive that stripped the Nuba tribes of their ancestral rights. Lands that had belonged to them for generations were now claimed by the government and the Arab elite.

The Nuba people were pushed further into the margins—politically, economically, and spiritually.

The law became a weapon. The land cried out, but no one listened.

This act did more than erase boundaries—it erased memory. It declared that what was not written did not exist, ignoring the oral traditions, the sacred markings, and the communal stewardship that had defined Nuba land ownership for centuries.

The law did not recognize the Nuba because it did not recognize justice. It did not recognize their memory. It did not recognize their dignity. It did not recognize their right to exist.

As the soil was seized, another force stirred beneath it—one that would deepen the wound and silence the world.

Oil, Oppression, and the Silence of the World
The Mountains Wept Oil, the People Bled Silence (1978-2005)

In 1978, the discovery of vast crude oil reserves in the region intensified the injustice. The Nuba Mountains became a target for exploitation. Successive regimes in Khartoum saw the land not as sacred heritage, but as a resource to be controlled.

The heartbeat of the mountains was drowned beneath the roar of extraction.

The oil fields brought pipelines, soldiers, and foreign contracts—but not schools, clinics, or roads for the Nuba. The wealth flowed outward, enriching the powerful and leaving the indigenous people in deeper poverty.

The mountains wept oil, but the people bled silence—and the silence was deeper than any wound.

What followed was a dark era of oppression, murder, and genocide—especially between 1983 and 1995. During these years, the world remained silent. The Sudanese government imposed a blockade on the Nuba Mountains, cutting off access to humanitarian aid and international observers.

The suffering was buried beneath silence; the cries vanished into the wind.

The silence was not empty—it was complicit. It echoed with the absence of mercy.

Entire villages were razed. Children died of hunger in caves. Mothers gave birth in darkness, without medicine or midwives. The Nuba clergy, once pillars of hope, were restricted for preaching peace.

The silence of the world became a second weapon—more enduring than bullets.

It wasn't until the early 2000s—between 2001 and 2005—that the international community began to respond. Pressure mounted on President Omar Hassan Al Bashir's regime. Sanctions were imposed. American diplomats negotiated access, and for the first time in decades, relief aid reached the Nuba people.

Hope arrived late, but it arrived. The caves opened and the wounded were seen.

The arrival of aid was not just logistical—it was spiritual. It reminded the Nuba that they were not forgotten. That their prayers had reached beyond the mountains. That mercy, though delayed, could still be born.

Yet even as aid trickled in, the deeper wound remained —a wound not of hunger alone, but of memory and dignity.

A Sacred Wound That Still Bleeds
Testimony as Memory

The scars remain. The injustice had already taken root. The land had been taken. The people had been wounded. And the silence had lasted too long.

History did not heal—it whispered its pain into every generation.

The Nuba do not seek revenge—they seek recognition. They do not ask for pity—they ask for partnership. Their resilience is not passive; it is active, creative, and sacred.

Each song sung in the mountains is a declaration of survival.

Yet the Nuba people endure. Their struggle is not merely political—it is sacred.

It is a cry for dignity, for memory, and for justice.

It is a prayer carved into stone, a hymn sung through suffering.

Their endurance is a theology of hope. It is a resistance that baptizes suffering into testimony. It is a witness that turns caves into cathedrals and wounds into wisdom.

This chapter is not just history—it is a call to remember, to speak, and to stand with those whose voices were buried beneath the rubble of war and silence.

To stand with the Nuba is to stand with truth.

To remember them is to restore what was taken.

To walk with the Nuba is to walk with the crucified – through the valley of silence, toward the dawn of resurrection.

It is to carry memory as a torch,

to restore dignity as a covenant, and

to proclaim peace as sacred witness.

Chapter Two

The Nuba Mountains Under Fire: A Declaration of War and a Testament of Hope

The Politics of Erasure: Sharia, Suppression, and the Seed of War

The Sudanese Civil War cast a long shadow over the Nuba people—an ancient, resilient community whose cultural heritage was scorched by political extremism. Their songs, dances, and languages, once freely expressed, were driven into silence. After repeated failures to impose sharia law in the Nuba Mountains, President Omar Hassan Al Bashir escalated repression, culminating in a formal declaration of war against the tribes of South Kordofan.

This action was not merely a political maneuver—it was an ideological purge. The imposition of sharia law was not only a legal framework but a tool of cultural domination. It sought to overwrite indigenous African cosmologies with a singular religious narrative, erasing ancestral memory and spiritual plurality. The Nuba, with their mosaic of faiths and traditions, became targets of a campaign that conflated religious purity with national identity.

To erase a people is to deny their right to remember. The politics of erasure weaponized law, language, and land. Schools were restructured to teach Arab-Islamic supremacy. Indigenous names were replaced. Rituals were banned. The Nuba Mountains, once a sanctuary of cultural diversity, were recast as a frontier of ideological conquest.

Timeline of Escalation

- 2007: Comprehensive Peace Agreement (CPA) invalidated
- April 24, 2011: President Omar Hassan Al Bashir's campaign speech in Muglat, South Kordofan
- June 5, 2011: War erupts in Umdoren village

Dates mark a descent from political maneuvering to tragedy. President Al Bashir's post-referendum declaration that northern Sudan would be Arab and Islamic signaled the erasure of indigenous African identities. The Sudan People's Liberation Army/Movement-North Sector (SPLA/M-NS) interpreted his speech as a declaration of war. When election results favored the National Congress Party (NCP) candidate, both parties claimed victory. The Sudanese Air Force surrounded Kadugli, and war erupted as peace delegates departed.

A War on Civilians, Culture, and Memory

This was not merely a war against soldiers—it was a war against civilians, culture, and memory.

- Airstrikes rained across the Nuba Mountains
- Villages, schools, hospitals, churches, mosques, farmland, and markets were bombed

The war was calibrated to dismantle the architecture of daily life. Bombs did not discriminate—they fell on places of worship, learning, healing, and trade. The destruction of schools was a strike against future generations. The targeting of churches and mosques was a desecration of spiritual refuge. The burning of farmland was a denial of sustenance and self-reliance.

Memory itself became a battleground. Oral histories were interrupted. Elders were silenced. Archives were destroyed.

Yet the Nuba refused to forget. In the face of annihilation, they became archivists of their own survival. Every act of endurance—planting a seed, singing a lullaby, carving a symbol—became a defiant act of remembrance.

Thousands fled to rocky caves, which became sanctuaries echoing with survival—children's whispers, mothers' prayers, and the thunder of warplanes. The cruelty was strategic, targeting the infrastructure of hope. Yet even in the caves, life persisted.

Women sowed seeds in hidden valleys. Elders became living libraries. The Nuba reimagined survival as sacred duty.

Songs in the Cave: The Spirit of Resistance

Despite suffering, the Nuba remained faithful and hopeful. Their songs of lament became hymns of resistance. Caves turned into cathedrals of defiance:

- Children wrote with charcoal on stone
- Mothers taught lullabies with coded hope
- Youths composed songs that traveled cave to cave

These songs were more than melodies—they were encrypted messages of resilience. The lullabies carried coded instructions for survival. The charcoal writings became maps of memory. The cave choirs echoed across valleys, stitching together a dispersed people with harmonies of hope.

In the absence of instruments, the body became the drum. In the absence of paper, stone became the scroll. In the absence of freedom, song became the sanctuary. The Nuba transformed suffering into liturgy, and caves into chapels of resistance.

Their resistance birthed new worship, identity, and community. The war tried to erase them—but they engraved themselves deeper into the land and legacy of Sudan.

Etched in Stone: A Prophetic Witness

The Nuba story is not frozen in time—it is a living testimony of hope under siege.

Their endurance is prophetic. As a spiritual witness, I affirm: the stones do not forget. Prayers whispered in caves rise like incense to heaven. Charcoal markings on granite became scripture for the suffering—each line a covenant of survival, each symbol a cry for justice. These inscriptions, born of anguish and faith, are not mere graffiti; they are sacred texts authored by the oppressed.

The caves became classrooms of resilience and sanctuaries of remembrance. In the absence of paper, stone became the archive. In the absence of freedom, memory became resistance. The Nuba inscribed their truth not for recognition alone, but for redemption. Their witness is not passive—it is active, generational, and divine.

To read these stones is to hear the heartbeat
of a people who refused to vanish.

Their testimony is carved into the land, echoing through time,
summoning us to remember, to honor, and to act.

Chapter Three

Faith in the Fire: The Church's Prophetic Witness in the Nuba Mountains

A Voice in the Wilderness: Seven Resolutions of Mercy and Justice

As bombs thundered over the Nuba Mountains and cries of the wounded rose from scorched earth, the Episcopal Church of South Sudan and Sudan did not retreat into silence. It rose—and I rose with it—bearing the Gospel into the fire, where faith meets affliction and mercy becomes mission.

"Faith in the Fire" is not a metaphor. It is a lived reality.

To understand the Church's response, we must first remember its roots. The Church Missionary Society (CMS) arrived in Omdurman, Sudan, in 1899. Pioneers such as Llewellyn Gwynne, Archibald Shaw, and Dr. Frank Harpur laid the foundation of the Episcopal Church of Sudan. Since then, the Church has stood as a pillar of peace across Sudan and South Sudan—supporting refugees, comforting the displaced, and advocating for justice in times of war.

But history does not remain in the past. The Church's legacy was refined in fire.

During the conflict between the Sudanese government and the Sudan People's Liberation Army/Movement-North Sector (SPLA/M-NS), dioceses under Government of Sudan control —Khartoum, Kadugli, El Obeid, Port Sudan, and Wad Medeni—were cut off from the Nuba Mountains. The Episcopal Church based in Juba, South Sudan, had to act. It had to become a defender and a voice for the Nuba people.

Under the leadership of His Grace Archbishop Dr. Daniel Deng Bul, longtime Chair of the Justice, Peace, and Reconciliation Commission, the Church convened an emergency meeting at the Provincial Headquarters. After prayerful deliberation, seven resolutions were adopted—not as bureaucracy, but as sacred response.

These became our liturgy of love:

1. Formation of a Nuba Taskforce

Bishop Paul Benjamin Yugusuk (Paolo) was unanimously appointed to chair the taskforce and officially delegated to oversee the Church's mission to the Nuba people. This was not a title—it was a sacred trust, a mantle of mercy. The Church entrusted him with its voice, its hands, and its heart.

2. Mobilization of Resources

All Saints Cathedral and provincial departments committed to purchasing emergency medicines and supplies for victims of aerial bombardments. The altar became a warehouse of compassion, the sanctuary a staging ground for mercy.

3. Advocacy and Lobbying

The Church pledged to advocate for the rights of the Nuba people and to lobby for humanitarian access to restricted areas. Our sermons became petitions. Our prayers became policy. Our witness became a bridge between heaven's justice and earth's suffering.

4. Provision of Humanitarian Aid

We committed to delivering medical relief and essential supplies to displaced families and wounded civilians. Each package of medicine carried more than relief - it carried the Church's promise: You are not forgotten.

5. Appeal to the Khartoum Government

A formal call was issued urging the government to cease aerial bombardments and open humanitarian corridors. Our appeal was pastoral—a cry of shepherds for their scattered flocks.

6. Counseling and Trauma Support

Plans were initiated to provide spiritual counseling and trauma healing for victims of human rights abuses. The Church became a balm for broken souls, a refuge for the shattered.

7. Encouragement through the Word of God

The Church resolved to uplift the Nuba people through scripture, prayer, and pastoral presence. In the valley of death, we carried the light of the Word. We did not preach escape—we preached endurance. We did not promise ease—we promised Emmanuel: God with us, even in the furnace of affliction.

A Mission of Mercy: Sent into the Mountains by Faith

And so, I was sent—not by ambition, but by calling.

The mountains awaited.

I humbly accepted this divine assignment as the first missionary sent to the Nuba Mountains after the independence of South Sudan on July 9, 2011. I had just witnessed the raising of our new Republic's flag—a moment born of the Comprehensive Peace Agreement (CPA).

I rejoiced to see my country free. Yet my heart ached, for the same agreement denied the Nuba Mountains and Blue Nile their promised popular consultation.

I went with a heart torn between celebration and sorrow, yet anchored in faith that God had not forgotten the Nuba.

Their cries rose like incense, and I knew heaven was listening.

Memory became my compass.

I walked in the footsteps of martyrs:

- Philip Abbas Ghabous - clergy and politician who stood for Nuba dignity.
- Butrus Tia Shukai - consecrated alongside my late father, Archbishop Benjamin Wani Yugusuk
- Mubarak Korkeil Khamis – first bishop of Kadugli
- Yousif Kuwa Mekki - SPLA/M revolutionary commander and politician
- And many other faithful servants etched in the memory of our Church

The moment of departure was not logistical—it was liturgical.

I stood before the altar at All Saints Cathedral, preparing to depart for the Nuba Mountains. The prayers of the faithful echoed in my heart.

This was not merely a mission—it was a divine summons to stand in the gap between suffering and hope.

This mission was not new—it was a continuation of a journey begun decades ago.

I recalled my calling as an evangelist to refugee camps in Ethiopia, Kenya, Uganda, Congo, and SPLA/M's liberated areas. For twenty years, it was hardship and struggle for the freedom of South Sudan and the Nuba Mountains.

Their pain was not abstract—it was personal. Their stories became my summons.

I remembered the testimonies of Nuba elders who had once walked proudly beside SPLM/A soldiers, believing in a future of dignity and freedom. Now, they were forgotten by politics, betrayed by silence, and left to endure the agony of bombardment and famine.

Their resilience stirred something deep within me—a holy fire that refused to be extinguished.

Silence was not an option. The Church's voice had to rise—not in judgment, but in mercy.

With conviction and compassion, I stepped forward—not alone but carried by prayer.

Where Heaven Meets the Mountains: Incarnate Gospel and Divine Presence

And there, in the heart of suffering, I witnessed something holy.

In the Nuba Mountains, the Gospel did not arrive wrapped in comfort—it arrived clothed in courage. It thundered from tents of the wounded, from altars turned into clinics, and from pulpits that dared to speak truth in the language of love.

Liberation, in this context, is not only political—it is spiritual. It is the breaking of silence, the healing of trauma, the lifting of forgotten voices. It is the Church becoming incarnate in suffering.

This is the Gospel among the Nuba—not distant, but incarnate. Not passive, but prophetic.

And the divine?

The divine is not absent from the battlefield. The divine is present in the trembling hands of volunteers, in the whispered prayers of the wounded, in the bold declarations of justice spoken from sanctuaries and shelters.

The divine is Emmanuel.
God with us—in tents, in tears, in trembling hands.

And so we remain: present, prophetic, and prayerful

Chapter Four

God's Divine Protection and Medical Provision

Protection in the Skies: The Emergency Landing at Lado Airstrip

In the shadow of war, the Church became a lifeline—its hands stretched across borders, bearing mercy. The Episcopal Church of South Sudan and Sudan Provincial Departments, together with the All Saints Cathedral congregations in Juba, generously contributed funds for emergency medicine and supplies for victims of air bombardments in the Nuba Mountains.

With these contributions, Rev. Emmanuel Lomoro, Coordinator of the Department of Education and Training and one of the heads of the provincial departments, was tasked with preparing emergency medical kits. He organized a carload of supplies and arranged for a chartered plane.

Early the next morning, we went to the airport and loaded the medical kits to travel to Kauda and deliver this lifeline to those suffering under relentless airstrikes.

I was heading into a war-torn region where the people of the Nuba Mountains faced daily bombardments. The regime had declared the area a no-humanitarian zone, banning all flights into Sudanese airspace.

I departed early. Soon after crossing into Sudanese airspace, my pilot spotted a Sudan Air Force plane trailing us—its intent unmistakable.

I committed my soul to God and prayed: Even if I die, the people of Nuba must live.

The pilot acted swiftly, making an emergency landing at a nearby airstrip called Lado, in Buram County. The engine was still roaring when she urged me to offload the medical kits quickly—she had to return immediately.

I unloaded the supplies as the military aircraft flew overhead, targeting our plane.

By God's grace, the pilot took off, flying low and fast toward the South Sudan border.

I was left alone at Lado Airstrip, surrounded by medical kits. Suddenly, three heavy rockets exploded in Lado village. One landed just meters from the supplies.

Now I was the target. I ran toward the rocky hills as the military plane circled above. I scrambled toward a large rock, praying aloud, "I recognize God's hand." In that moment, fear bowed to faith.

The rock became my altar, the sky my sanctuary—where fear bowed to faith and heaven drew near.

The plane flew past. I was safe—for now.

While hiding, I heard voices beckoning from the side of the mountain. Though afraid, I took a step of faith and approached them.

They welcomed me warmly and led me into a cave carved by God's hand to protect His people, the Nuba. Their eyes held stories of survival—etched in silence, spoken in embrace.

It reminded me of David's refuge in the Cave of Adullam, where the broken and oppressed gathered, and God forged a community of courage. This cave, too, was a sanctuary of divine mercy.

To my astonishment, the cave was vast, sheltering hundreds. Inside, people who had taken refuge from daily bombardments sipped coffee and tea, shared meals, and prepared food.

They explained that every day, from 10:00 am to 1:00 pm, military planes—Antonovs—hover over the Nuba Mountains. During those hours, villagers flee to the cave and return home only after the planes retreat to Khartoum or El Obeid.

Week after week, month after month.

I stayed with them. Exhausted and humbled, I lay on the rocky floor and slept. The cave's silence cradled me. In its depths, I felt the heartbeat of a people who refused to surrender.

The cave had cradled our fears, but now the wind whispered a new command. As the Antonovs retreated and the sun pierced the mountain's veil, the time for hiding gave way to healing.

What God had sheltered, He now summoned. The mission stirred again—not beneath the rock, but among the wounded.

Provision and Healing Medicine Amid the Rubble

At exactly 1:00 pm, the Antonovs retreated, and the cave emptied. A few young men remained and helped me carry the medical kits to Lado Health Unit, two kilometers away. They made three trips, balancing the cartons on their heads.

Upon arriving, I saw dozens wounded by the airstrikes—some lying on the floor, others being carried in, alive and dead. The horror of the plane attack faded as I witnessed the real suffering of the Nuba people. Their wounds spoke louder than the rockets.

I prayed to God for protection and peace to prevail. My mission on this first day was filled with danger and sorrow.

The village chief and the Lado Health Unit director noticed the cartons labeled "Emergency Medical Kits - Destination: Kauda, Nuba Mountains." They approached me, introduced themselves, and expressed sympathy for what I had endured. I shared my mission to deliver the medical kits to Kauda for victims of airstrikes and to stand with the people of Nuba in their difficulties.

They thanked the Episcopal Church for standing with the people of Nuba Mountain during this very difficult time.

They asked if I could provide some medical supplies to treat the wounded. Seeing the pain around me, I authorized them to take five large cartons of emergency medical kits.

Treatment began immediately. The kits, once destined for Kauda, became instruments of mercy—rerouted by grace. God had rerouted healing.

While treatment continued, I asked the chief to take me to the bomb sites. We walked together and saw destroyed homes. A woman had died in her house—beyond recognition.

I met displaced women from Kurungu village. They had fled airstrikes only to find the bombardment followed them across the Nuba Mountains. I shared God's message with them and prayed for protection, provision, and peace. They wept as I left.

By evening, all patients had received care. The health unit grew calm.

As I prepared to rest on the hospital floor, a Sudan People's Liberation Movement/Army - Northern Sector (SPLM/A-NS) truck smeared with mud entered the compound. I overheard the driver say he had come to park and would travel to Kauda early in the morning.

I recognized God's provision in the humility of the truck—it was no coincidence. I approached the driver, Choko'do, and explained my mission.
He immediately agreed to help and asked that the medical kits be loaded. We loaded the kits together.

In Choko'do's smile, I saw God's provision.

I lay down again on the health unit floor—this time with the assurance that I would reach Kauda the next day.

Benediction in the Rubble: A Night of Providence and Promise

That night, on the health unit floor, I reflected on God's divine plan:

- He orchestrated the emergency landing to deliver medicine to Lado village.
- He protected me and the villagers in the cave.
- He used the donation to treat hundreds of wounded.
- He sent me to console the bereaved.
- He provided free transport to Kauda through Choko'do and the SPLM/A-NS truck.

Each step was a thread in God's tapestry of mercy. Each encounter, a verse in His unfolding song of hope. Each hardship, a doorway to divine provision.

Though I slept hungry, I rested in God's providence.

Though the floor was hard, His promises were soft beneath me.

Though the night was long, His presence was near.

In the silence, I heard the echo of ancient prayers—
of prophets who fled into caves,
of widows who gave their last meal,
of shepherds who followed stars through the dark.

This was not a night of despair. It was a vigil of trust. A benediction whispered not from pulpit but from the rubble of war and the breath of the wounded.

The cave, the kits, the kindness of strangers—all bore witness to a God who does not abandon His people, a God who walks through fire, flies through danger, and sleeps beside the broken.

By morning, the mission would continue. But that night, heaven had already come near.

The courage I witnessed in the caves and villages will not be in vain.

When that dawn breaks, the Nuba shall rise—not in fear, but in praise. Their songs will be the sunrise. Their healing, the hymn. Their survival, the sermon.

And the rubble shall remember:

God was here.

Chapter 5

Sheltered by Grace: Healing Amid the Ruins of Kurchi

Fleeing the Fury: Mercy in the Sky

We rose early, hearts lifted in prayer, and journeyed toward Kauda, unaware that divine protection would soon be our only shield. The road was dusty and unforgiving, winding through dry terrain and scattered rocks.

After hours of travel, we reached a small trading center called Abu Lila. There, we paused to stretch our weary bodies and drink water—simple acts of relief after a long, uncomfortable ride. But the peace was short-lived.

Not long after leaving Abu Lila, while still en route to Kauda, an Antonov army plane suddenly appeared in the sky, roaring like a beast unchained from the heavens. Its thunder split the sky. Without warning, it began shooting at our convoy.

The drivers, alert and courageous, veered off the road and parked the trucks beneath trees, seeking camouflage from the aerial assault. We heard the thunderous sound of bombardment ahead—though distant, it echoed with terror. When the bombing finally ceased, we exhaled, hearts still pounding, clinging to the grace that had spared us.

We arrived in Kurchi, a town nestled among mountains, only to find devastation. The airstrikes had left behind a trail of sorrow and destruction. Lives had been lost, families torn apart, and the wounded lay scattered. Fear gripped the air like a storm cloud refusing to lift. It hung over every face, every cry, every silence.

Panic was everywhere. Children cried. Mothers searched for loved ones. Elders sat in stunned silence.

We entered the compound of the Nuba Relief and Rehabilitation Development Organization (NRRDO), where we were received with warmth and compassion. Kurchi became a place of refuge—a sanctuary amid the chaos. There, I was finally served a meal—the first I had eaten in two days since leaving Juba. As I tasted the food, a wave of gratitude washed over me. It was not just nourishment for the body, but a balm for the soul.

After the meal, I walked through the ruins. I saw homes reduced to ashes, farms destroyed, livestock killed. Women and children ran in fear, their eyes wide with trauma. My heart broke as I witnessed the suffering etched into every corner of this wounded land.

In Lado, I saw the worst destruction I had ever witnessed in a single day—human suffering and property loss beyond imagination. I cannot begin to fathom the condition of other places I have yet to visit, including Kauda, the administrative headquarters of the Sudan People's Liberation Movement/ Army - Northern Sector (SPLM/ A-NS).

I lifted my voice in prayer for Kurchi.

I called upon the Lord to protect His people, to bring healing to broken bodies, and peace to troubled hearts.

I prayed for divine intervention—
let mercy flow like the river of life through the scorched valley.

The dust of destruction had barely settled when a new call emerged—not to flee, but to serve. The ruins did not silence our calling; they amplified it. In the brokenness, we heard the whisper of purpose. In the wake of sorrow, we did not retreat into despair.

Instead, we stepped forward, led by grace, into the heart of suffering. What awaited us was not only pain, but the sacred invitation to be healers in a wounded land. Though the Antonov's fury left Kurchi trembling, it was not the final word.

Beneath the weight of sorrow, a deeper grace stirred—one that would carry us from the shadow of destruction into the light of restoration.

> Where bombs had fallen, prayers now rose.
> Where sorrow had settled, mercy began to bloom.

What followed was not merely survival, but a sacred unfolding of mercy, where healing took root in the valley of pain.

Tending the Wounded: Healing in the Valley

The next morning, I was taken to the Kurchi Health Centre. What I saw there will remain with me forever. Dozens of injured people lay on the floor—no beds, no medicine, no bandages.

Only pain, waiting for mercy. Some had been suffering for weeks without treatment. Their wounds were raw, their spirits weary.

Moved by compassion, I donated emergency medical kits to the Kurchi Health Centre. The staff, though exhausted, sprang into action. They began treating the wounded immediately, and lives were saved that very day.

I walked among the patients, praying for each one by name. I laid hands on the wounded, consecrating each broken body with whispered prayers, trusting God to mend what man could not.

I prayed for the medical personnel and the administration, that they might be strengthened in their mission of mercy.

As the sun set over Kurchi, the echoes of suffering gave way to whispers of hope.

That evening, we began our journey to Kauda. The road was tedious, and we passed several places devastated by airstrikes. The entire Nuba Mountains region bore the scars of destruction—evidence of a campaign that felt like human cleansing.

As darkness fell, I prayed silently in the car, asking for God's protection and an end to the violence.

We arrived at night and were welcomed once again at the NRRDO compound, where I spent the night. I meditated on the faithfulness of God and His mighty hand in this mission. I gave thanks for the completion of the third leg of this noble journey.

That night, in my room at the NRRDO compound, I reflected on God's divine plan. He had:

- Protected us from the airstrikes on the way to Kauda
- Enabled me to provide medicine and medical supplies to Kurchi Health Centre
- Touched and healed those injured by the bombings
- Provided military vehicles to escort me free of charge to critical hotspots in need of medical relief and supplies

Rising from Ashes: Mercy in the Midst of Ruin

In the midst of destruction, God's hand was evident—not only in shielding us from harm but in guiding us to be instruments of healing. Kurchi, though wounded, became a place of refuge and renewal. The cries of the injured, the resilience of the medical staff, and the prayers lifted in faith remind us that even in war, mercy flows.

And in the valley of death, we saw life stir again—carried by grace, sustained by love.

From the ashes of despair, a new resolve was born. Mercy did not merely descend from above—it rose from within the hearts of the suffering.

I saw it in the eyes of a nurse who had not slept for days yet continued to treat the wounded with tenderness. I saw it in the hands of a child who shared her last piece of bread with another. I saw it in the quiet strength of elders who, though displaced, still offered wisdom and comfort to the young.

This mercy was not passive. It was active, defiant against the cruelty of war. It rebuilt what bombs had shattered. It stitched together the torn fabric of community. It whispered to the broken: "You are not forgotten. You are not alone."

In Kurchi, we did not merely survive—we began to rise.

The ruins became sacred ground, not because they were untouched by violence, but because they were touched by grace.

Every prayer uttered, every wound tended, every act of kindness became a stone in the altar of mercy.

Let this testimony be a lamp in dark places, a call to compassion, and a witness to the God who shelters, heals, and sends us forth.

In Kurchi, amid the ashes, we found the altar of mercy.

Truly, we were sheltered by grace—and called to shelter others.

Chapter Six

Shielded by Grace: The Miracle in Kauda – A Testimony Forged in Fire

The Unexploded Bomb: A Divine Veto on Death

On a quiet Sunday morning in Kauda, I walked toward the Church of Christ, unaware that the day would soon erupt in violence. Suddenly, I saw people fleeing toward trenches. Alarmed, I too sought shelter. Just as I began to run, a MiG military aircraft dropped a rocket mere meters in front of me.

Miraculously, it did not explode.

While other rockets tore through homes and hearts, the one meant for me lay silent—a divine veto against death, a heavenly refusal to let violence have the final word.

I stood there, shaken. I did not know whether to weep or worship, but I knew I had been spared for a reason. I had witnessed firsthand the violation of human dignity and the wanton destruction of property and vital infrastructure. Yet in that moment of terror, I also witnessed divine shielding.

Though trembling, I pressed on—driven by the call to worship and the need to bear witness.

That rocket, inert and lifeless, became a symbol of grace. It was not merely a failed weapon; it was heaven's message: not today. In the midst of chaos, God had drawn a line the enemy could not cross. I did not escape the war; I was enveloped in a miracle.

From the silence of the rocket to the sound of praise, we crossed a threshold—from terror to testimony.

Worship After the Strike: Songs Louder Than Sirens

After the aircraft had flown away and the airstrikes ceased, I continued to the church to join the congregation. Some were still emerging from trenches; others had gone home, their Sunday service disrupted.

With the few who remained, worship began. These were not just worshippers—they were warriors of faith, defying despair with every note sung.

Pastor Muktar Abalo, the pastor in charge of the Church of Christ, noticed me and kindly invited me to greet the congregation. I shared the purpose of my visit to the Nuba Mountains and testified to God's protection throughout my journey from Lado to Kauda.

I did not merely recall a verse—I embodied a truth. I stood in the storm yet was not swept away. I walked through fire yet was not consumed. My refuge was not in walls, but in the unseen arms that held me.

The congregation was deeply moved—not only by God's protection over me, but by the miracle of the unexploded bomb. They began to praise God and thank Him for His shield over our lives.

Shielded by grace, we worshiped not beneath the shadow of war, but beneath the shelter of the Almighty.

In that humble church, surrounded by echoes of violence, we lifted our voices in defiance of fear. The sanctuary became a battlefield of praise, where hymns were our weapons and hope our shield. Each hymn was a declaration: we are not forsaken.

What began as a moment of survival became a monument of testimony—a fortress built not of stone, but of song.

Fortress in the Firestorm: Praise in the Valley of Death

In Kauda, where the skies roared with violence and the earth trembled beneath falling bombs, God's protection became more than a promise—it became a lived miracle. The unexploded rocket was not merely a technical failure; it was a divine interruption, a shield extended over a servant walking in faith.

That Sunday, worship rose from the ashes. The few who gathered did so not in fear, but in defiance of despair. Their songs declared that even when the world crumbles around us, we are not alone.

This moment in Kauda is etched not only in memory, but in testimony. It reminds us that even in war zones, God walks with His people. His protection is not always the absence of danger, but the presence of peace, purpose, and praise in its midst.

The miracle in Kauda is a chapter in a larger story—a story of a people who refuse to be silenced, a church that refuses to be scattered, and a God who refuses to abandon His own.

In the valley of death, we found a fortress. In the line of fire, we found grace.

In the trembling silence of an unexploded bomb, we heard the whisper of divine mercy.

We did not flee—we sang.

We did not fall—we stood.

We did not perish—we praised.

Blessing in the Rubble: Grace That Refuses to Retreat

The miracle in Kauda did not end with the silence of an unexploded bomb—it echoed through every hymn, every trembling voice that chose praise over panic. In the shadow of war, we found the shelter of worship. In the afterm ath of violence, we built a sanctuary of song.

This chapter is not merely a memory—it is a blessing. A reminder that grace does not retreat when rockets fall. It advances, shields, and sings. It turns trenches into altars and ruins into testimonies.

Kauda stands as sacred ground, not because it was spared from war, but because it bore witness to mercy. The unexploded rocket was not the end—it was the beginning of a deeper call: to worship louder than sirens, to stand firmer than fear, and to testify even when the world trembles.

We were not shielded to remain silent.

We were spared to speak, to sing, to stand.

Chapter Seven

Mercy in the Midst of War
Medicine, Prayer, and Presence at Luwery Hospital

A Pilgrimage of Mercy: Bearing Hope into Suffering

The day after my arrival in Kauda, Rev. Luka Bulus—who had journeyed ahead as part of our delegation—joined me as we ascended to witness the suffering endured by the Nuba people. Our mission was both strategic and sacred: visits to hospitals, humanitarian outposts, social gatherings, and military sites, each chosen for its spiritual and symbolic weight. We carried emergency medical supplies—and a message of divine solidarity.

It was no mere logistical undertaking; it was a pilgrimage of mercy. Every step was steeped in prayer. Every encounter was shaped by the conviction that compassion must walk where suffering dwells. We came not as saviors, but as servants—bearing witness, bearing burdens, bearing hope.

From this sacred ascent, we arrived at a place where pain and perseverance meet—a hospital transformed into both crucible and cathedral.

Luwery Hospital: Where Pain and Perseverance Meet

Luwery Hospital, perched on a hill like a weary sentinel, greeted us with scenes of profound anguish. Civilian and military casualties lay side by side—wounds untreated, spirits worn thin. Once a sanctuary of healing, the hospital now echoed with the cries of the wounded and the quiet desperation of nurses working with almost no medicine, no food, and no hope.

Their testimonies were harrowing:

infections treated with prayer alone

wounds dressed with torn cloth

lives slipping away for lack of basic supplies.

One nurse, her hands trembling, whispered, "We do what we can, but sometimes all we have is faith."

The air in those corridors was thick with pain—yet pierced by the resilience of those who refused to abandon their post. Their courage was not loud, but it was unyielding. They were the unsung saints of this war-torn land.

In response to this suffering, we extended our hands—not with plenty, but with purpose. What we carried may have been small, but its meaning was vast.

Mercy in Motion: The Gift of Emergency Kits

In the face of such scarcity, we delivered emergency kits—modest in quantity, rich in compassion. Each kit handed over was a silent prayer, a gesture of mercy that said: "You are not forgotten."

The hospital staff received them with trembling hands and grateful hearts, knowing that even a small act of provision can mean the difference between life and death. One medical assistant, weary from days without rest, clutched a kit and said, "This is more than medicine. It is hope."

These were not just supplies—they were sacraments of solidarity. Yet even as we offered physical aid, we knew that healing must also come from heaven. And so we turned to prayer—the balm that never runs dry.

Prayer as Balm: Intercession Amid Ruins

Beyond physical aid, we offered what no shortage can diminish: prayer. I led intercessions for the injured, the medical staff, and the families torn by conflict. In the stillness of that moment, a divine whisper was heard: "This suffering will usher in a better tomorrow." It was not a promise of ease, but of redemption—that through the valley of pain, a new dawn will rise.

The prayers echoed through the halls like incense—rising, lingering, sanctifying the air. Lifting the weary. Anchoring the broken. Some wepr. Some smiled faintly. All were reminded that heaven had not turned its face away.

And then, amid the wounded, one voice rose—not in anger, but in longing. A soldier's plea became a moment of grace.

A Soldier's Longing: Dignity in a Bar of Soap

Among the wounded was a South Sudanese soldier—his body broken, his spirit longing for home. He asked not for arms, but for embrace. Not for vengeance, but for return.

Moved by his humility, I knelt beside him and offered more than aid—I offered dignity. A prayer for healing. A shirt, a trouser, a pair of sandals, and a bar of soap from my own bag. A promise that he was not alone.

His eyes filled with tears—not from pain, but from the recognition that he was seen. Not as a casualty, but as a child of God. In that moment, the war faded, and what remained was the sacredness of human connection.

Entrusted to Return: Mercy as Mandate

As we prepared to leave Luwery, the weight of what we had seen did not crush us—it commissioned us. We carried not just memories, but a mandate.

In Kauda, amid the ruins and resilience, we learned again that the gospel is not only preached—it is lived. It is lived in the offering of soap and sandals . . . in the kneeling beside the broken . . . in the refusal to turn away from suffering.

Luwery Hospital was not just a place of pain—it was a sanctuary of perseverance. And our presence there, however brief, became a sacrament of solidarity.

We left not with triumph, but with testimony:

> That even in the valley of death, mercy walks beside us, a rod and staff of comfort
>
> That even in the absence of medicine, prayer prevails—healing not only wounds, but hearts.
>
> That even in war, love endures.

And so we went forth—not emptied, but entrusted. Entrusted with the stories of the Nuba people.Entrusted with the sacred duty to remember, to speak, and to return.

For in every act of mercy, heaven draws near.

And in every step of solidarity, the Gospel is lived.

Chapter Eight

Gidel: A Hospital of Hope Amid Horror

In the heart of the Nuba Mountains, where war has scorched the land and scarred its people, Gidel Catholic Hospital stands as a fragile sanctuary. What I witnessed there was both harrowing and holy.

A Scene of Suffering and Survival

When we arrived at Gidel Catholic Hospital, the air was thick with anguish. Sister Angelina Nyakuru, a Ugandan Comboni sister and head nurse, welcomed us into a crucible of crisis. Built to serve 200 patients, the hospital was now sheltering more than 500 casualties—men, women, and children wounded by relentless airstrikes across the Nuba Mountains.

Patients lay on floors, verandahs, corridors, tents, and even beneath trees. More than 20 surgeries were being performed daily, stretching every resource to its breaking point. As I moved among the wounded, praying and listening to their stories, an Antonov aircraft roared overhead, reigniting trauma and fear. Yet even in their suffering, the people clung to hope that one day, they would rise again.

Amid this valley of pain, I encountered the quiet heroism of those who refused to abandon their post.

The hospital was not merely overcrowded—it was overwhelmed. Every corner bore witness to human fragility and divine endurance. The wounded lay not in sterile wards but on bare earth and concrete, their bodies broken, their spirits trembling, yet somehow still reaching for life.

The roar of the Antonov was not just a sound—it was a memory, a threat, a wound reopened. And yet, in the eyes of the suffering, I saw something deeper than fear: I saw resilience. I saw faith. I saw a people who refused to be erased.

This scene was not just one of medical crisis—it was a sacred space of survival. A place where

> pain met prayer
> where despair met defiance, and
> where the human spirit, though battered, refused to die.

Let the world understand: Gidel is not a statistic. It is a sanctuary. And every soul within it is a testimony to the power of hope in the shadow of horror.

The Healers: Courage Amid Crisis

Inside the operating theater, I met Dr. Tom Catena, a U.S. physician and the only expatriate doctor remaining at Gidel. Alongside Sister Angelina and three Sudanese nurses, he was performing surgeries on shattered limbs and life-threatening injuries. All other qualified doctors had been evacuated, leaving this small team to carry the weight ofan entire region's suffering.

I prayed for Dr. Tom and his team, whose courage and sacrifice stood as a living testament to compassion in the darkest of times. I witnessed a man undergoing surgery for a broken leg, and later walked through the wards, offering prayers for those who had already been operated on.

But even the bravest hands cannot heal without tools. The cries of the wounded echoed a deeper plea.

What I saw in that theater was more than medical skill—it was sacred defiance. These healers stood between death and life, refusing to surrender to despair. Their hands stitched torn flesh, but their presence stitched together the soul of a broken community.

Dr. Tom's quiet endurance, Sister Angelina's unwavering tenderness, and the Sudanese nurses' tireless labor were not just acts of service—they were acts of love. In a place where bombs fall and resources vanish, they remained. Not because it was safe, but because it was right.

Their courage is not loud—it was steady. It did not seek applause—it sought healing. And in their witness, we saw the Gospel made flesh: mercy in motion, compassion under fire, hope with a heartbeat.

Let the world know their names. Let the Church honor their sacrifice. For in the story of Gidel, the healers are the prophets —speaking through scalpels, bandages, and prayers.

The Cry for Help

The hospital's needs were staggering. Dozens of patients had lost limbs, and the list of urgent requirements was long:

- Trained medical personnel
- Hospital beds
- Dry food supplies (sorghum, oil, sugar, salt)
- Essential medicines
- Medical equipment
- Soaps and detergents
- Plastic sheets, mats, and mosquito nets
- Clothing for displaced patients
- Tents to serve as makeshift wards

This was not a list—it was a lament. Each item spoke of lives suspended between survival and despair. A missing hospital bed meant a child slept on the ground. A lack of medicine meant a wound may fester. A shortage of food meant healing was delayed. These needs were not logistical—they were moral.

Despite the overwhelming burden, I held fast to the belief that with God, all things are possible. We handed over the remaining emergency medical kit, trusting that even small acts of mercy can ignite great hope.

And among the wounded, the smallest voices carried the deepest sorrow. Gidel was not asking for luxury. It was pleading for dignity. The staff were not demanding comfort—they were begging for tools to save lives. And the patients, many of them children, were not seeking miracles—

they were praying for mercy. Let this cry reach beyond the mountains. Let it stir churches, clinics, and communities across the globe. For when we respond to Gidel's cry, we do more than deliver supplies—we deliver hope. And in doing so, we become part of the healing.

The Children of War

Among the many faces I encountered, three children remain etched in my heart.

Jacomy Gebril, a 12-year-old boy from Tes village, had traveled from Khartoum to visit his grandmother. When the bombings began, his friends shouted in their native tongue for him to lie down. But Jacomy, raised in the city, did not understand. He stood — and a piece of shrapnel tore off his hand. I appealed for him not to return to the village and sought a school for him through the kindness of well-wishers. I later learned he had been taken to another station.

I also met a four-year-old girl in urgent need of surgery that could not be performed in the Nuba Mountains. Her fragile body bore the weight of a war she could not comprehend.

Another girl, suffering from tetanus, was placed in an isolated room. Sister Angelina advised us not to enter, as she was dying. I prayed for her from outside, lifting her soul like incense toward heaven.

These children are not statistics; they are sacred lives, calling us to envision a better tomorrow. Each child carries a story that pierces the heart and demands a response. Their wounds are not only physical—they are spiritual, emotional, and generational. In their eyes, we see the cost of silence. In their cries, we hear the urgency of justice.

Jacomy's severed hand is a symbol of interrupted innocence. The dying girl behind the closed door is a reminder of the fragility of life in forgotten places. And the four-year-old awaiting surgery speaks for every child whose future hangs in the balance.

We must not look away. These children are the prophets of our time—bearing witness to suffering, yet still capable of hope. To serve them is to honor the image of God in its most vulnerable form.

Let every school, every clinic, every church, and every heart rise to protect them. For in the healing of these children, we heal the soul of a wounded land.

A Vision for Healing

As I walked through the hospital, the burden of war pressed heavily on my spirit. Gidel stood as the only major hospital in the region with a functioning theater. Even as another Antonov flew overhead, I envisioned a future where Gidel is fully equipped, staffed with qualified personnel, and able to treat the children of Nuba with the care and dignity they deserve.

That afternoon, we returned to the Nuba Relief and Rehabilitation Development Organization (NRRDO) compound. The humanitarian needs of the Nuba people were vast—calling for selfless hearts and urgent action.

I left Gidel with a renewed conviction: the Church must rise to advocate, to lobby, and to stand in solidarity with the resilient people of Nuba. Their journey toward freedom and dignity demands our unwavering support.

This vision is not merely logistical—it is spiritual. It is a call to restore what war has tried to erase: the sanctity of life, the dignity of care, and the promise of healing. Gidel must become more than a hospital; it must become a beacon of mercy, a center of resilience, and a sanctuary of hope for generations to come.

Imagine a Gidel where no child is turned away, where every wound is met with skilled hands and compassionate hearts, where the cries of the suffering are answered not with silence, but with solidarity. This is the future we must build—not alone, but together.

Let every partner, every church, every humanitarian agency hear this call: equip Gidel, empower its healers, and uplift the Nuba people. For in doing so, we do not simply mend bodies—we restore humanity.

A Call to Compassionate Action

That afternoon, I sat in silence, reflecting on the suffering I had witnessed. The cries of the wounded, the courage of the caregivers, and the innocent faces of children like Jacomy and the little girl in need of surgery stirred something deep within me. The dying girl. The restless wards. Dr. Tom and his team.

This was no longer just a mission—it was a divine calling. We must act. We must speak. We must heal. I resolved to rally support, engage with partners, and speak boldly for the voiceless. For in the heart of Gidel, amidst the ruins of war, I saw not only pain but the flicker of hope.

And I knew: we must fan that flame into a fire of healing, justice, and peace. To remain silent is to betray the wounded. To delay is to risk another child's life. The Church must rise—not only in prayer, but in prophetic action. We must become the hands that carry medicine, the voices that challenge indifference, and the hearts that embrace the broken.

Let every parish, every mission, every believer hear this call: Gidel needs us. The Nuba people need us. Let our compassion be practical—mobilizing resources, amplifying their stories, and building coalitions of mercy.

For in every shattered limb, in every whispered prayer, in every child's cry,
God is calling us to respond.

Not tomorrow. Today.

Chapter Nine

Divine Appointment: The Church's Witness in the Nuba Mountains

The Church as Bridge and Beacon

I met with the Inter-Church Committee (ICC) under the chairmanship of Rev. Muktar Abalo, one of the few clergy of the Church of God who remained with his congregation throughout the war. I briefed the committee on my mission to the Nuba Mountains. They shared the critical role the ICC had played during the conflict—liaising with NGOs and encouraging Christian leadership to remain steadfast in the face of adversity.

They expressed a deep need for prayer and partnership with the Episcopal Church of South Sudan and Sudan to support the suffering people of Nuba. We were united in our conviction that the Church was instrumental to the future of Nuba, with a vital role in ensuring lasting peace, freedom, and prosperity in a land where people depend wholly on the grace of God.

From this sacred dialogue of unity and purpose, our journey continued deeper into the heart of the Nuba Mountains, where the echoes of war were met by the unwavering resilience of faith.

A Garrison of Gratitude and Grief

My companion Rev. Luka Bulus and I paid a courtesy visit to the Sudan People's Liberation Movement/Army - North Sector (SPLM/A-NS) commanders at Luwery. Rev. Luka formally introduced me to Major General Izzat Kuku, a prominent military figure and personal commander based in Luwery, Kauda. Known primarily for his leadership role in the SPLA-N in the Nuba Mountains, General Kuku welcomed us with warmth and respect.
I shared the purpose of my mission and the reason for visiting their headquarters. I extended heartfelt appreciation to Choko'do, a devoted

SPLM/A-NS driver who had transported critical medical kits and ensured my safe passage to Kauda during a moment of great urgency. His courage and commitment reflect the quiet strength that sustains our people.

General Kuku commended the Church's provision of emergency medical kits and congratulated South Sudan on its independence. He emphasized the importance of lobbying and advocacy in response to the ongoing airstrikes that had devastated lives, property, crops, and livestock.

As we spoke, I reflected on a future where the Nuba Mountains would rise above conflict—a time when its people would enjoy freedom, security, and the abundant resources God has bestowed upon them. I reminded them that the Nuba had fought alongside South Sudanese, and though the Khartoum regime denied them the right to popular consultation, their struggle was not in vain. I prayed for God's protection over them and encouraged them to stand firm in their pursuit of justice.

With these solemn reflections still stirring in my heart, we pressed onward to Kauda, where the voices of leadership bore witness to the suffering of the people.

From the Commissioner's Desk: A Plea for Justice

After meeting General Kuku, we proceeded to Kauda to meet Hon. Kamal Al-Nur Daoud, a former colonel and Commissioner of Heiban County under the Sudan People's Liberation Movement-North (SPLM-N). He shared the dire humanitarian crisis unfolding in Kauda, overwhelmed by the rising number of Internally Displaced Persons (IDPs).

The Commissioner pleaded for urgent humanitarian relief and intensified advocacy for equal human rights for the Nuba tribes. He encouraged the Episcopal Church to raise a prophetic voice on behalf of the Nuba people and to expose the atrocities committed by the Sudan Government.

He affirmed that the Church's voice could be stronger than that of politicians if it spoke globally on behalf of the oppressed. "We are one people in South Kordofan and South Sudan," he said. "The Church must lead in advocacy and mediation."

I left the meeting encouraged and prayerful that God would enable the people of Nuba to rebuild their communities and live in peace and dignity.

Women ofthe Mountain: Voices of Resolve

That evening, we met with the Women's League. The gathering was led by:

- Hon. Former Minister of Social, Child Welfare, and Religious Affairs from South Kordofan
- Advisor to the Governor
- Members of the State Parliament
- Commissioner of Heiban
- Youth Representative for the Right to Popular Consultation

It was deeply inspiring to witness the women of Nuba preparing to rebuild their broken communities and lead their people toward prosperity.

Together, we resolved the following recommendations:

- Lobby for the cessation of air bombardments and excessive force against civilians b y the Sudan Air Force
- Establish a "no-fly zone" to allow only humanitarian flights
- Urge the international community to pressure the President Al Bashir-led government to stop the violence
- Address the humanitarian blockade that has left the Nuba Mountains closed to the outside world, predicting a severe shortage of food and basic items within a month
- Call on the UN to recognize the atrocities and loss of life as genocide or ethnic cleansing
- Advocate for the UN Security Council to invoke Article 7, allowing the use of force to protect civilians, rather than Article 6, which only permits monitoring and reporting.

This meeting renewed my hope in a peaceful and prosperous future for the Nuba people. With the voices of these courageous women still echoing in our spirits, we joined hands with those laboring on the frontlines of relief—the humanitarian community striving to meet urgent needs.

The Consortium of Compassion

We attended a crucial meeting with the Non-Governmental Organizations (NGOs) Consortium chaired by the Commissioner of the Sudan Relief and Rehabilitation Commission (SRRC). The meeting included ten organizations and representatives from the Catholic Diocese of El Obeid. The consortium had formed a strong lobby group on June 9, 2011. Participating organizations included:

1. Save the Children
2. Nuba Relief and Rehabilitation Development Organization (NRRDO)
3. Norwegian Church Aid (NCA)
4. Pact Sudan
5. Concern
6. MC Scotland
7. Samaritan's Purse (SP)
8. Kodi
9. Sudan Relief and Rehabilitation Commission (SRRC)
10. Red Crescent

Meeting recommendations:

- License an SRRC office in Juba to coordinate activities
- Allocate the refugee camp at Itang in Unity State for displaced Nuba people, with urgent needs for education and health programs
- Address the loss of personnel and lack of operational resources—fuel, tires, and lubricants—which had grounded their vehicles
- Highlight the rising number of IDPs, which had reached 425,933 and continued to grow

- Urge immediate provision of food and medical supplies. The World Food Program had reduced monthly rations from 12kg to 6kg per person due to escalating displacement

The consortium was left in charge of food distribution but warned that reserves would only last one month. I was convinced that both the humanitarian sector and the Church had the capacity to help the Nuba people overcome their afflictions.

Divine Threads: A Journey Woven by Grace

I had seen the dire needs of the Nuba people. I had covered more ground than I had expected. That day, I pondered the hand of God in my emergency landing at Lado airstrip. I saw the purpose of my trip as divinely ordered.

The cave, a sanctuary carved by suffering, became a wellspring of grace. It led me to hospitals in desperate need of medical supplies, to injured soldiers longing for care, to key policymakers and commanders, and ultimately to the displaced people scattered across the Nuba Mountains.

I witnessed the horrific suffering of children, women, and victims of airstrikes. Though devastated by the emotional, spiritual, and physical needs of the Nuba people, I remained optimistic.

One day, these tragedies will be no more.

One day, the people of Nuba will flourish.

Chapter Ten

Caring for the Nuba Oppressed

Visit to the Internally Displaced Persons (IDPs) Camp in Kauda

We entered the sacred threshold of suffering—the women's centre in Kauda —where the scent of ash lingered, and the displaced clung to hope amid the ruins of war.

We sat with them, listened to their testimonies, and bore witness to their pain. Their faces carried the weight of sorrow and injustice.

One woman, her voice trembling with grief, asked: "Why is Bashir bombing us? Why civilians and not the army?"

Their eyes were filled with bitterness and anguish. I had no answers to offer—only a listening heart.

They recounted the horrors they had endured: the loss of loved ones, the trauma of displacement, and the chilling words attributed to President Bashir, who allegedly branded Nubians as 'atheists' and vowed to eliminate them. Yet in the bombings, both Christians and Muslims had perished. It was inhuman. It was unacceptable.

At the IDP camp, the needs were glaring and urgent. These displaced families were in a desperate state. I witnessed their immediate needs:

- Food to quiet their hunger
- Shelter to protect their children
- Clean water to quench their thirst
- Medicine to ease their pain
- Clothing to restore their dignity

Despite their suffering, I saw resilience.

A quiet hope flickered within them—the hope that one day they would triumph, living in peace and abundance in a free land, no longer terrified by the sound of planes overhead.

Each time the Antonov roared above, the mountain became their sanctuary. They fled not from fear alone, but from memory—from the echo of bombs that had already stolen too much.

On their behalf, I made a humanitarian appeal for urgent relief aid.

Later, we shared lunch with the delegation that had accompanied me. Around that table, we held deep discussions about our shared responsibility in building a free, peaceful, and prosperous Nuba community.

Visit to Lado IDPs Camps and Homecoming Farewell

The Episcopal Church of South Sudan had been searching for us, fearing the worst. Communication was severed. Kauda had become silent on the map. Flights could not reach the Nuba Mountains, and Kauda was inaccessible.

We received word from Juba that a flight would arrive the following day at Lado airstrip, where we had previously made an emergency landing. We were advised to reach Lado as early as possible for evacuation.

With the kind assistance of NRRDO, we were provided a vehicle to make the journey. We decided to combine our homecoming with a visit to the IDPs in Lado, whom I had briefly met during a previous trip. Together with Rev. Luka Bulus, we departed early in the morning and arrived in the evening.

Upon arrival, we met the local chief and visited the displaced families. Many had fled the relentless bombardments in Kurungu locality, leaving behind homes, families, and livestock. The village chiefs had opened their hearts and homes to host them, yet the suffering was immense. Hunger gnawed at them—there was no food.

We spoke with several of them, mostly women. We encouraged them with the Word of God. We also held counseling sessions with grieving families, offering comfort, prayer, and the Word of God.

The humanitarian needs of the Nuba people were overwhelming.

I witnessed firsthand the devastation caused by airstrikes. The destruction was said to have stretched across:

- Buram locality
- Kadugli locality
- Deleng locality
- Umdoren locality
- Haiban-Kauda locality
- Delami locality
- Jau locality

And yet, in the valley of anguish, God whispers a deeper truth: The tears of the Nuba people will not be wasted.

Their endurance will birth peace. Their pain will become prophecy.

Farewell and Homecoming

Farewell is never a forgetting—it is a carrying.

As we departed from the soil of Kauda and Lado, we did not leave behind the suffering. We carried it with us, like sacred embers glowing in the heart of the Church.

The journey from anguish to testimony is not measured in miles, but in memory.

In the waving hands beneath the aircraft, I saw not only relief but a silent commissioning:

"Go, and tell the world what you have seen."

The following morning, the time had come to return to Juba. We traveled through the night from Kauda to Lado village, having completed our visit to the IDPs and fulfilled our mission.

At 9:00 a.m., the aircraft landed safely. The same captain who had previously left me with medicine kits under heavy bombardment was overjoyed to see me again. She urged us to board quickly, as the threat of an approaching Antonov or MiG aircraft loomed.

We boarded and departed from the Lado airstrip.

As the aircraft lifted from Lado, hands waved below, blessing us with silent prayers. Their joy was not in our leaving, but in our survival. Their farewell was a benediction

Arrival and Testimony Presentation at the Episcopal Church Headquarters

We arrived safely at Juba International Airport in the afternoon. Upon arrival, I was taken directly to the Episcopal Church Headquarters, where the Archbishop and heads of departments warmly welcomed me.

I presented a comprehensive report detailing my mission to the Nuba Mountains. I conveyed the tragic and urgent plight of the Nuba people—caught amidst killings, destruction, and profound suffering. I also testified to the miraculous escape in Lado, the divine provision and protection we experienced, and the healing hand of God that sustained us.

I informed the Archbishop of the deep appreciation expressed by the people of Nuba, the churches, and SPLM/A-NS.

Rev. Emmanuel Lomoro, one of the heads of the Episcopal Provincial Departments, gave thanks to God for the successful mission and commended the courage with which it was undertaken.

Archbishop Dr. Daniel Deng appreciated the mission report and thanked God for our safe return and the spiritual impact of the journey. He then directed his administration to organize a public briefing to be held at All Saints Cathedral.

The Episcopal Church's role in sending medical supplies to victims of airstrikes in the Nuba Mountains was nothing short of prophetic. It was a living testimony of the Church's calling to stand with the suffering. In those moments, the protection and provision of God were not abstract—they were real, tangible, and deeply felt.

Benediction of the Broken: A Closing Witness

The benediction of the broken is not a conclusion—it is a calling.

In the dust of Kauda and Lado, we found not despair but sacred ground. The cries of the displaced became liturgy. Their endurance became Scripture.

The Church must not only preach peace—it must walk into the fire and return with testimony. This mission was not ours alone. It was the Spirit's movement through wounded places, whispering:

"Blessed are those who mourn, for they shall be comforted."

As the dust of Kauda and Lado settled behind us, the echoes of suffering and resilience remained. The cries of the displaced, the prayers whispered beneath bomb-laden skies, and the silent strength of the Nuba people followed us like a sacred refrain. Their stories were not left behind—they journeyed with us, etched into our hearts and into the mission of the Church.

The sacred threshold of suffering has become a sanctuary of testimony. And the mission of the Church—etched with the tears of the Nuba—continues.

For every broken body, there is a healing promise.

For every silenced cry, a future song.

The benediction of the broken is not pity – it is power. It is the Church's vow to remember, to respond, and to rebuild. It is the Spirit's breath over scorched earth, saying:

"From these ashes, I will raise beauty."

So let the Church go forth –

Not with polished sermons, but with pierced hearts. Not with comfort alone, but with courage.

For the broken are not forgotten.

They are the prophets of tomorrow.

Chapter Eleven

The Ripple from the Cave: A Nation Under God's Testimony

A Cry Heard in Juba - When Silence Became a Summons

The cathedral was full. From NGOs to church leaders, Nuba intellectuals, and provincial department heads—all gathered in solemn anticipation. Archbishop Daniel Deng Bul stood among us. The Episcopal Church of South Sudan and Sudan, in partnership with the Nuba Relief and Rehabilitation Development Organization (NRRDO), convened this urgent briefing. The air was heavy with grief yet charged with purpose.

On the screen, a PowerPoint presentation unfolded horrors too great for words:

- Mass killings of civilians and animals
- Destruction of homes, schools, health centers, churches, mosques, markets, and farms
- Images of suffering etched into banners and hearts alike

The silence in the room was not emptiness—it was reverence. A collective mourning. A sacred pause.

The cave was not chosen—it was given. In the moment of terror, it became a refuge. In the absence of systems, it became a sanctuary. And in the silence of suffering, it became a place where testimony was born.

From that cave in Lado, a ripple began. It was not loud, but it was holy. It carried the breath of survival, the whisper of mercy, and the cry of a people not forgotten. That ripple reached Juba, where banners bore witness and prayers were lifted. It reached Sydney, where diaspora hearts were stirred. And it continues to move—through testimonies, through gatherings, through the sacred work of remembrance.

The ripple from the cave is not just a story. It is a summons. A call to conscience. A movement of faith and justice. It reminds us that even in the darkest places, God is present. And from the ashes of war, a cathedral of testimony can rise.

The Testimony of Lado

At the end, I stood to share one testimony—one ripple from the cave.

In Lado, I escaped an airstrike by the mercy of God. The people sheltered me in a cave, where medicine was miraculously provided. Treatment came not from systems, but from compassion. God arranged a truck to carry me to Kauda.

Though the situation was dire, the miracle in Lado stirred praise from the congregation. God had not abandoned His people.

Lado was not a battlefield—it was a place of hiding, of healing, of holy intervention. When the airstrike came, I was spared—not by strategy, but by grace. The people took me in, not as a stranger, but as a brother. In the cave, medicine appeared —not from clinics, but from compassion. It was as if heaven bent low to touch the wounded.

A truck was arranged. A way was made. And I reached Kauda, carried not by logistics, but by love.

This testimony is not mine alone. It belongs to the people who sheltered me. To the prayers that sustained me. To the God who did not abandon us.

When I shared this in the cathedral, the congregation did not merely listen—they praised. Because in the midst of genocide, God had moved. And the testimony of Lado became a song of survival.

A Call to Action

We appealed to NGOs for urgent intervention. We called upon the Church to pray for the people of Nuba. We thanked NRRDO for their unwavering support—especially Nejwa Musa Kunda, the Executive Director, whose partnership was a lifeline.

The Provincial Department and All Saints Cathedral congregation offered generous contributions, both spiritual and material. The Sudan People's Liberation Movement/Army North Sector (SPLM/A NS) for their support and the liberation struggle.

Testimony demands response. It is not a passive recounting—it is a prophetic invitation.

In Juba, we called upon NGOs to act swiftly. We urged the Church to pray fervently. We thanked NRRDO for standing with the people of Nuba, especially Nejwa Musa Kunda, whose leadership was a lifeline in the storm.

We recognized the contributions of:

- Humanitarian partners who refused to look away
- The Episcopal Church and All Saints Cathedral, who gave both prayer and provision
- The SPLM/A North Sector, who stood with the liberation struggle

This call to action was not political—it was pastoral. It was civic. It was sacred. Because when a people suffer, silence is complicity. And when a testimony is shared, it must be met with solidarity.

Bearing Witness - From Banners to Prayer

Outside the cathedral, large banners bore witness to the genocide—images that revealed the magnitude of suffering in the Nuba Mountains. For two weeks, people came. They stood. They wept. They prayed. They shared the story with others. The ripple from the cave became a wave of awareness.

Outside the cathedral, the truth could not be ignored. Banners stretched across the compound, bearing images of suffering too great for words. They were not decorations—they were declarations.

For two weeks, people came. They did not rush. They stood. They wept. They prayed. They bore witness.

Some brought candles. Others brought tears. All brought presence.

The ripple from the cave had become a wave of awareness. It moved through hearts, through conversations, through communities. It reminded us that testimony is not just spoken—it is seen. It is felt. It is shared.

And in that sacred space, banners became altars. Silence became prayer. And grief became a form of resistance.

Testimony from Australia: A Diaspora Encounter with the Nuba Community in Sydney (2019)

In 2019, I was delegated by His Grace Justin Badi Arama, Archbishop and Primate of the Episcopal Church of South Sudan, to attend the GAFCON Primates Meeting in Australia. Following the gathering, I embarked on a pastoral visit across Sydney, Melbourne, Brisbane, and Perth—cities that cradle diverse communities and stories of migration, resilience, and faith.

While in Sydney, I requested a meeting with the Nuba diaspora community. Upon contacting the chairperson, a gathering was graciously organized. The turnout was remarkable. The chair introduced me as a bishop from South Sudan, carrying fresh testimony from the heart of Nuba Mountains—a mission marked by suffering, survival, and divine intervention.

I took the stage, not as a guest but as a witness. I shared the painful truth of genocide, the enduring hand of God upon the people of Nuba, and my personal testimony from Kurchi—where God protected us amid danger and where healing flowed in Kuechi like a stream in the desert. I spoke of the women and children, the silent cries, and the urgent need for prayer and advocacy. I urged the diaspora to speak to their second countries, to lift the veil on what is unfolding back home.

The room was attentive. Hearts were stirred. Many wept quietly, others nodded in solemn agreement. My testimony moved the audience, not because of eloquence, but because of the merciful power of God that continues to sustain His people. The chair offered a vote of thanks not only to me, but to all who came, united in purpose and prayer.

Where Testimony Was Born: A Ripple That Reached the World

From the banners outside to the prayers within, the testimony of Lado began to stir hearts. It was no longer just my story—it had become a communal witness. And now, it must become a global one.

The cave that called my name was not merely a shelter—it was a sanctuary. A place where testimony was born from terror, and hope rose from the ashes. The ripple from that cave reached Juba, and from Juba, it must reach the world.

Let this chapter be a call to conscience.

Let it stir prayer, provoke action, and awaken solidarity.

Let it remind us: even in the darkest valleys, God is present. And the cave becomes a cathedral of testimony.

The ripple from the cave is not confined to geography—it is a spiritual current. It carries the memory of suffering and the miracle of survival. It speaks not only to the Nuba people, but to every soul who has endured injustice and cried out for mercy.

In Juba, it was banners. In Sydney, it was prayer. In Kauda, it was healing. E ach place received the ripple differently, yet all were drawn into its sacred rhythm. The testimony of Lado became a bridge —between war and worship, between silence and speech, between local pain and global awareness.

This is how testimony travels: not by force, but by faith. Not by broadcast, but by bearing witness. It moves through hearts willing to listen, through communities willing to act, through churches willing to pray.

The cave was not the end—it was the beginning. The ripple was not a whisper—it was a wave.

And the world must now receive it—not as news, but as sacred truth.

Testimony from the Nuba Women's Prayer Conference - Sydney

Following the Nuba community meeting, a powerful prayer conference was held in Sydney, and I was honored to be invited. We were warmly welcomed, and the gathering was filled with the presence of God. The main speaker—a woman of deep faith—preached the Word of God with such power and conviction that the entire assembly was moved. Her message of encouragement blessed us profoundly.

During the program, a special guest was introduced: a bishop from South Sudan, originally from the Nuba Mountains. Though I was not one of the scheduled speakers, I was graciously given the opportunity to greet the conference and share a few words.

I introduced myself, spoke of my journey to Australia, and shared my mission to the Nuba Mountains. I gave a report on the current situation in Nuba—the suffering, the genocide, and the urgent need for advocacy and prayer. As I narrated the pain of the people and the devastating effects of war, I also testified to God's protection on the way to Kurciti, and the provision of medicine and healing.

As I spoke, the people rose in worship, lifting their hands in adoration to God for His goodness and faithfulness. It was a sacred moment of unity and praise.

I urged the diaspora women to speak to their second countries—to lift the veil on what is unfolding back home. Their voices, I reminded them, are bridges between continents and cries from the cave. They carry the power to awaken compassion in places of influence.

This gathering was more than a conference—it was a consecrated assembly of intercessors. The women did not merely listen; they responded with tears, with prayer, with prophetic conviction. Their worship became a form of resistance. Their praise became a declaration that God has not forsaken the Nuba people.

In their prayers, I heard echoes of Kauda and Kurciti. In their songs, I felt the heartbeat of those still in the mountains. The diaspora had not forgotten—they had remembered with power.

I thanked the conference organizers for the opportunity to speak and for their open hearts. The gathering concluded with joyful presentations by children and other activities that celebrated our shared faith and hope.

In that room, testimony became intercession.

Pain became praise.

And the ripple from the cave found yet another shore.

Chapter Twelve

From the Mountains to the Desert: Rebirth of War, Renewal of Witness

The Silence That Speaks

Years have passed since my feet last touched the rugged soil of the Nuba Mountains. Though the air raids have ceased and a fragile calm now rests upon the hills, the wounds of injustice remain open. The people of Nuba still carry the weight of marginalization, their dignity tested by decades of neglect and violence. The SPLA-North has reclaimed much of the region, save for a few government-held towns like Kadugli and Deleng. Yet even in relative peace, the scars of war whisper through the valleys.

The silence is not empty—it speaks. It speaks of graves without names, of children who learned to run before they learned to read, of mothers who buried hope beneath the soil. It speaks of churches turned to rubble and prayers uttered beneath the shadow of jets.

The Nuba conflict did not begin with the airstrikes of 2011. Its roots stretch back to the 1980s, when the people of the mountains first rose against systemic oppression. Their struggle has spanned generations—marked by displacement, resistance, and resilience. And still, the mountains remember.

The Desert Burns

As the mountains mourned, the desert burned.

While the Nuba people endured decades of marginalization, another tragedy was unfolding in Sudan's western deserts. In 2003, the Darfur genocide began—years before the aerial bombardments of Nuba gained international attention. President Omar Hassan Al-Bashir, seeking to crush rebellion, turned his fury westward.

The government armed tribal militias—later known as the Janjaweed—and unleashed them upon the people of Darfur.

What followed was not merely conflict, but a campaign of terror:

- Villages turned to ash
- Women defiled
- Children left to mourn alone

The desert became a furnace of grief. The cries of Darfur echoed across the sands, unanswered. The world watched, but mercy delayed is mercy denied. The Church must not delay.

From Janjaweed to RSF: Power Rebranded

From the ashes of the Janjaweed rose a new force: the Rapid Support Forces (RSF). Heavily armed and state-sanctioned, the RSF became the government's instrument of control—not only in Darfur, but across Sudan. Their commanders gained wealth and influence, their power growing even as the regime that birthed them began to crumble.

Power changed its name, but not its nature. The uniform was new, but the violence familiar. The RSF inherited the legacy of impunity, cloaked in legitimacy. They patrolled cities, guarded borders, and silenced dissent. Their rise was not a rebirth of order—but a rebranding of fear.

The Cry for Freedom

But tyranny, though vast, cannot silence a nation's soul.

In 2019, the Sudanese people—young and old, Muslim and Christian, rich and poor—rose in defiance. They filled the streets with chants of freedom, demanding an end to Bashir's 30-year rule. Their courage shook the foundations of tyranny. The military, sensing the tide, removed Bashir from power. A transitional government was formed, and for a moment, hope flickered.

President Bashir—the architect of war in the Nuba Mountains, the man who unleashed genocide through airstrikes and destroyed the future of generations—was finally behind bars in Kober Prison, Khartoum. The same president who empowered the Janjaweed militias to commit crimes against humanity in Darfur now sat in custody.

There was talk of justice. The new leadership under General Abdel Fattah al-Burhan pledged to hand Bashir over to the International Criminal Court (ICC). But justice, like peace, is fragile—easily promised, rarely delivered.

The cry for freedom was not just political—it was spiritual. It was the soul of a nation groaning for redemption.

Between Hope and Betrayal

But the road to freedom is never straight. Between hope and betrayal lies the valley of compromise. And in that valley, old enemies find new weapons.

The revolution birthed dreams, but also dilemmas. Promises were made in the language of peace but broken in the dialect of power. The people who danced in the streets now weep in the shadows. The Church must walk with them—not as spectators, but as shepherds.

Alliance Shattered, Nation Torn

In the aftermath, the RSF and the Sudanese Armed Forces (SAF) entered into an uneasy alliance. They shared power, but not trust. Beneath the surface, rivalry festered.

In April 2023, that rivalry erupted into open war. The RSF and SAF turned their weapons on each other, plunging Sudan into a new civil war.

Darfur, once again, became a battlefield. Ethnic violence surged.

Cities were razed.

Families displaced.

The cycle of suffering deepened.

The war that began in the mountains has now engulfed the nation. Sudan is now a battlefield — thousands have died, properties destroyed, and millions displaced. Many have sought refuge in South Sudan and neighboring countries.

The alliance was not a covenant — it was a ceasefire between wolves. And when it broke, the sheep suffered.

Let Memory Become Mercy

This chapter is not merely a chronicle of conflict — it is a call to remembrance. The pain of Nuba, the agony of Darfur, the courage of the protestors, and the betrayal of peace must not be forgotten. As a servant of Christ, called to bear witness to sorrow and hope alike, I write so that the world may see — and seeing, may act.

Let the mountains speak. Let the desert testify. Let the Church rise — not in silence, but in solidarity.

Let every pulpit echo the cries of the displaced.

Let every prayer carry the names of the forgotten.

Let every act of mercy become a seed of peace.

Let memory become mercy.

Let mercy become movement.

Let movement become mission.

Chapter Thirteen

The Land Remembers: A Pilgrimage Through Pain and Promise

Return to the Mountains: A Pastoral Journey of Memory and Witness

There are places where memory walks ahead of you, waiting to be met again.

Arrival and Awakening

After many years, I returned to the Nuba Mountains—a land that once held my footsteps in fear and faith. This time, I journeyed not alone, but with Bishop Andudu Adam Elnil, diocesan bishop of Kadugli, Episcopal Church of Sudan, and his wife, Rev. Jalila. Though now residing in the United States, they remain deeply rooted in the ministry of the Church. Our mission was pastoral, but it became a pilgrimage of memory, healing, and renewed witness.

We flew from Juba to Yida, a town in the Pariang Administrative Area, Unity State, near the border with Sudan and adjacent to the Nuba Mountains. Unlike my first visit—when I was dropped into unfamiliar terrain, unaware of the geography or destination—this journey was marked by clarity.

We entered Jau, a border town on the southeastern frontier between Sudan and South Sudan, passed the junction touching Tobo County, and continued until we reached Lado.

Memory Rekindled in Lado and Kurchi

In Lado, I paused to visit the village, the health unit, and the airstrip. The image of Lado, once fragmented in my memory, came into focus with striking clarity. From there, we journeyed to Abu Laila for a brief stopover, then pressed on beside the long mountain range—around the place where the Antonov once spotted us and our driver branched off in hiding—until we reached Kurchi.

The terrain was mountainous and different from what I remembered—rugged, yet resilient.

The following day, we visited the diocesan offices. Bishop Andudu has built a dignified structure with reliable internet and a welcoming residence. These facilities did not exist during the time of bombardment. Their presence now is a testament to perseverance and faith.

We also were taken to the construction site of Grace Boarding Secondary School—a monumental undertaking funded by Relay Trust UK. I remembered bringing secondary school teachers from Uganda who had come to teach. Later, we returned to Bishop Andudu's home.

Seeds of Education and Faith

The next day, we traveled to Tobo, where we visited the church nursery school. We met the teachers and support staff. The pupils sang for us. The nursery school lacked even the basics—no building, benches, blackboard, or learning materials.

That evening, we joined the congregation in Tobo for a fellowship gathering filled with prayer and encouragement. The prayers were held at the home of the church preacher. They welcomed us warmly, and together we praised God, shared testimonies, and prayed for their needs.

Our journey concluded with a return to Yida and then back to Juba.

This time, I carried with me a full picture of the Nuba Mountains. The only place I did not revisit was Kauda—where I once escaped a MiG rocket on my way to church, while delivering medicine and meeting with the commander, commissioner, inter-church leaders, women's league, NGOs, and hospitals in Luwery and Gidel.

The Unfinished Struggle

One truth must be spoken plainly: though years have passed, the suffering in the Nuba Mountains remains. The situation is still dire. Citizen services are limited. Infrastructure remains destroyed. Some areas continue to face bombardment—now targeting SPLA-North positions. The promises of the Comprehensive Peace Agreement (CPA), especially the Popular Consultation, were never fulfilled.

This book remains relevant because the pain has not ceased. The people of Nuba still cry for justice, for dignity, for peace. But I believe—this time, God will grant them total freedom.

- Let the land remember.
- Let the Church not forget.
- Let the world not turn away.
- Together, we must rise in unity until justice prevails.

Strengthening the Church in Doulabi

Less than a month after our first mission, I returned with Bishop Andudu to Kurchi. Our hearts were still burning with the memory of the cave and the cries of the faithful. We revisited Tobo and the nursery school, where seeds of hope had already begun to sprout. This time, I brought along scholastic materials as a gift to the school.

At the Tobo County Hall, we organized a full-day teaching workshop titled "Firm Gospel Foundation: From Creation to Christ." More than 100 believers and their pastors attended, including many new converts. The teaching was received with gratitude and reverence. The Spirit moved among us, affirming the urgency of grounding this young church in truth.

While I taught in Tobo, Bishop Andudu journeyed to one of his churches in the village of Doulabi (also known as Al Reika). He returned in the evening, and together we traveled back to Kurchi. But my heart was stirred—I felt compelled to visit the church in Reka. Bishop Andudu agreed, affirming that the congregation was newly established and in need of encouragement.

A Nation in Crisis

During this period, the RSF clashed with the Sudan Armed Forces (SAF) in Kadugli. The civil situation became tense. Essential commodities vanished. Kadugli was under siege. The government loosened long-standing restrictions on movement to SPLA-N territories, and thousands of civilians fled to the Nuba Mountains.

God heard the prayers of His suffering people and led them back to their ancestral land. Just as airstrikes once ravaged the mountains, they ceased. Just as Darfur endured unspeakable crimes, the war was abandoned. Now, the whole country is engulfed in conflict—but God has heard the prayers of Darfurians too.

During our visit to Tobo, our training and pastoral outreach coincided with the influx of thousands of internally displaced persons (IDPs) from Kadugli and Khartoum. Bishop Andudu and I visited three IDP camps, each sheltering over 50,000 people.

The situation was dire—no food, no water, no shelter, no medicine. This generation of Nuba had grown up in towns like Khartoum, Kadugli, and El Obeid. They had never known displacement. Many survived on wild fruits like coconut. Children died—unaccustomed to hardship, and without access to medicine.

We held talks with camp authorities and addressed thousands of IDPs, assuring them that God hears their prayers and will provide for their needs. The interview was broadcast, and soon after, Samaritan's Purse, the World Food Programme, and others responded.

Though they suffered greatly, God not only fed them—He freed them from the hand of their oppressors.

Living the Gospel

On Sunday, we first stopped in Tobo for a brief prayer, then proceeded to Doulabi (Al Reika). We found the congregation already gathered, with others still arriving. While we were being welcomed, I witnessed a painful scene—a man striking his son with a cane. The child wept bitterly. I later learned the boy had tried to attend church. My heart ached. In that moment, I knew the gospel must not only be preached—it must be lived, defended, and made safe for the smallest among us.

Though I had intended to teach the full gospel foundation, I was led to focus on one lesson: God and His Plan of Salvation. The message was received with grace and attentiveness. The Spirit confirmed its timing. A testimony was shared by the school director of Tobo, who had attended the earlier teaching. He said it was moving and had strengthened their faith.

After the preaching, the church administration raised concerns: the need for naming the church, a permanent building, and theological training for their members. Bishop Andudu responded with pastoral clarity. I also decided to offer a scholarship for one individual to study theology at Kaleyo International Bible Institute in Western Kenya.

We concluded with a word of prayer and returned to Kurchi—hearts full, mission extended.

Divine Timing in Yida

The following day, we traveled to Yida. A dust storm had reduced visibility, and that same day, a plane crash occurred near the Yida airstrip. Our flight was delayed for several days. We contacted Samaritan's Purse, which had a scheduled flight the next day. By grace, the flight arrived, and we were able to travel.

Rev. Jalila was scheduled to fly to the USA that same day. Upon arrival at Juba International Airport, all passengers had already checked in with Ethiopian Airlines. We approached the counter just as it was closing, and Rev. Jalila was graciously checked in.

We give thanks for the timely provision of the Samaritan's Purse flight—without it, she would have missed her journey.

We arrived safely in Juba, carrying with us the seeds of faith and leadership planted in Doulabi (Al Reika).

In that moment of delay and danger, we were reminded that divine interruptions are often divine interventions. The dust storm that grounded us became the veil through which God's provision was revealed. The crash that shook the region did not claim our lives. The closed gate at the airport opened just in time. These were not coincidences—they were confirmations. In the wilderness of uncertainty, God made a way. In the dust, He wrote mercy. In the delay, He delivered grace.

We did not just return to Juba—we returned with a testimony of divine timing, carrying not only seeds of leadership, but the fragrance of God's faithfulness. We returned with a deeper understanding: that the God who calls us to serve also orchestrates our steps. That even in the chaos of conflict and the unpredictability of travel, His timing is perfect. We carried with us not only the memory of mission, but the assurance that every journey taken in faith is held in His hands.

A Promise Fulfilled

In the months that followed, the church in Doulabi (Al Reika) sent a student to pursue theological studies in Kenya. Philimon Kuku enrolled in the diploma program in Biblical Studies and Christian Leadership at Kaleyo International Bible Institute. He graduated successfully and returned to Reka, where he continues to preach the Word of God with conviction and grace.

Philimon's return is not just a personal triumph—it is a seed of transformation planted in the soil of suffering.

His journey is a living parable of hope fulfilled. From the dust of displacement to the discipline of study, from the hunger for the Word to the harvest of ministry—Philimon embodies the promise that God does not forget the faithful. His voice now echoes through the hills of Reka, not as a visitor, but as a shepherd.

His presence is a quiet revolution: a reminder that theological education is not a luxury for the privileged, but a necessity for the persecuted. In him, the prayers of a village, the vision of a bishop, and the faith of a people converge. And through him, the gospel walks again among the Nuba—stronger, deeper, and rooted in truth.

The church in Doulabi has not only gained a preacher—it has gained a witness:

Philimon's life is a testimony

that the seeds sown in hardship can bloom into leadership

that the Word of God, when planted in good soil,
will bear fruit in season

that the promise of transformation
—spoken in prayer, carried in faith, and fulfilled in obedience—
will never return void.

Chapter Fourteen

A Historic Pastoral Visit to the Nuba Mountains: Consecration, Communion, and the Birth of Hope

Enduring Faith Amidst Displacement

When the center collapses, the margins become the altar. In the wake of national upheaval, the Church has not retreated—it has re-rooted. As Khartoum emptied of its Christian leaders, the Episcopal Church of Sudan found sanctuary in Port Sudan, where Archbishop Ezekiel Kondo Kuku Kumir continues his ministry with unwavering resolve. His presence there is not merely administrative—it is pastoral, prophetic, and profoundly symbolic. The prayers of the global Anglican communion have become a canopy over this displaced leadership, reminding us that exile does not erase calling.

As Christian leaders flee Khartoum and scatter across Sudan and neighboring countries—South Sudan, Uganda, Egypt, and beyond—Archbishop Kondo remains steadfast. He and his family have relocated to Port Sudan, now the provisional capital of the Government, where he faithfully continues his archbishopric duties.

Nationally, regionally, and globally, the church —including the Episcopal Church of South Sudan, the Global South Fellowship of Anglican Churches (GSFA), and the Global Fellowship of Confessing Anglicans (GAFCON)—has been fervently praying for Archbishop Kondo, his wife Mama Surya, and all who have sustained the church's continuity in Port Sudan.

A Mission of Encouragement and Consecration

Every consecration is a covenant—between heaven and earth, memory and mission. In a moment marked by divine timing, Archbishop Kondo set forth on a pastoral journey to the Nuba Mountains. His mission was twofold: to inaugurate the newly formed Diocese of Heiban and to consecrate its first bishop, El Sir Hassan Kuku. This act was not simply liturgical—it was a declaration of hope, a planting of spiritual infrastructure in soil long tilled by suffering. My own invitation from Bishop Andudu Adam Alnial was a call to witness and participate in this sacred unfolding.

Honored by Bishop Andudu's invitation, I embraced the call without hesitation. As a missionary to the Nuba Mountains and as my second province, I accepted immediately.

Upon informing Archbishop Kondo of my intention to join his delegation, he graciously welcomed me. Bishop Andudu and I traveled ahead to Yida, where we awaited the archbishop's arrival. He was warmly received by Bishop Andudu and the diocesan delegation, and we spent the night at the Samaritan's Purse compound.

Among the delegation were Mama Surya, who ministered in her capacity as matron of the Mothers' Union of the Province; Bishop Samaan Farajalla Mahdi of Wad Medeni; and Rev. Ludia Botrus Shokai, daughter of the pioneering Bishop of Nubian heritage and founding shepherd of the Diocese of Omdurman. Rev. Ludia joined us from the UK, where she serves with the Diocese of Leeds.

Reception in Kurchi and Heiban

Where the people gather, the Spirit dances.

Our arrival in Kurchi and later in Heiban was met with a reception that transcended protocol—it was worship in motion. Choirs sang, youth ran alongside our convoy, and elders lifted prayers of thanksgiving. These gatherings were not mere formalities; they were expressions of communal joy, resilience, and reverence. The Church was not only present—it was alive, radiant, and ready to receive the mantle of new leadership.The next day, we journeyed to Kurchi, the diocesan headquarters, and were met by a vast congregation—government officials, NGOs, and believers all gathered to glimpse the archbishop. A joyous and reverent welcome followed, filled with choir praises, worship, and heartfelt speeches.

Each delegate was introduced and greeted the congregation. Archbishop Kondo, guest of honor, brought greetings from the Christian community in Sudan and shared the purpose of his pastoral visit: to encourage believers and consecrate the new diocesan bishop. He closed with prayer and benediction.

After spending the night at Bishop Andudu's residence, we traveled with an even larger delegation to Heiban. Upon arrival, we were received with great joy and thanksgiving. Youth accompanied our convoy with jubilant procession, a living psalm of welcome, running alongside our vehicles until we reached the cathedral. That evening, we were again welcomed with speeches and songs of praise. Gratitude overflowed as we gave thanks for journeying mercies and sacred fellowship.

Consecration and Vision

The consecration of Bishop El Sir Hassan Kuku was more than a ceremony—it was a spiritual commissioning. Surrounded by bishops, dignitaries, and believers from across the Nuba Mountains, the new diocese was born in prayer, song, and prophetic vision. Bishop El Sir Hassan's message was clear: the Diocese of Heiban would be a place of healing, teaching, and transformation. His vision echoed the heartbeat of the region—a longing for dignity, discipleship, and durable peace.

The following day, we held a pastors' retreat that included Bishop-elect El Sir Hassan and offered foundational teachings in Anglicanism, followed by a consecration rehearsal.

On Sunday, the consecration day, we welcomed a delegation from the Sudan People's Liberation Movement/Army-North Sector, including H.E. Jodgod Mukuar Marda, Deputy Chairman of SPLM-N; the Secretary General of SPLM-N; the Governor of South Kordofan; the Commissioners of Kauda and Heiban; and other dignitaries. Their attendance affirmed the enduring partnership between spiritual leadership and civic responsibility in the Nuba Mountains. Church delegations from across the region, including Kadugli, also joined.

With the support of Bishop Andudu Adam Alnial of Kadugli, BishopSamaan Farajalla Mahdi of Wad Medeni, Bishop Hassan James Osman (Assistant Bishop of Kadugli), and myself as Archbishop of Central Equatoria Internal Province in the Episcopal Church of South Sudan, Archbishop and Primate Ezekiel Kondo Kuku Kumir inaugurated the Diocese of Heiban and consecrated Bishop El Sir Hassan Kuku. The new bishop shared his vision for the diocese, inspiring hope and commitment.

Before departing for an important meeting in Juba, I was given the opportunity to greet the congregation. I expressed deep gratitude to Bishop Andudu for his invitation and to Archbishop Kondo for including me in this historic mission. I congratulated Bishop El Sir Hassan and pledged to partner with him in strengthening diocesan capacity for effective ministry and service delivery.

To consecrate is to kindle—

to light a fire that others may carry.

Chapter Fifteen

Global Solidarity with the Nuba Mountains: A Covenant of Restoration and Hope

From Crisis to Commitment
A Call to Conscience, A Journey of Restoration

The Nuba crisis is not merely a humanitarian concern—it is a moral summons to the world. It reveals the cost of silence and the urgency of solidarity. As we reflect on the pain endured, we must now pivot toward purposeful action. This pivot demands not only resources, but reverence—for the dignity of the Nuba people and the sacredness of their resilience.

From the ashes of displacement and despair, we are called to rise—not merely with aid, but with allegiance to justice. This commitment is not transactional; it is transformational. It asks us to walk with the Nuba people, not as saviors, but as stewards of shared humanity. In every school rebuilt, every clinic staffed, and every story preserved, we declare: the Nuba are not forgotten. Their resilience is our responsibility.

The following developmental activities offer a roadmap for transformation, rooted in compassion, justice, and unity.

Developmental Activities to Stand with Nuba

Education and Healing

- Education, Schools, and Scholarships
  Build and rehabilitate schools across the Nuba Mountains. Provide scholarships for displaced and vulnerable children. Train teachers in trauma-informed pedagogy and peace education. Even amid conflict, education must remain a sanctuary of hope.

- Mobile Health Clinics and Training Hubs
  Deploy mobile units staffed with trained local health workers to reach remote areas. Establish training centers to build local capacity in trauma care, maternal health, and disease prevention.

- Faith-Based Trauma Healing Centers
  Establish safe spaces for spiritual and psychological healing, led by trained clergy and counselors, integrating scripture and communal storytelling.

Peacebuilding and Civic Renewal

- Peace Education and Conflict Resolution Institutes
  Create community-based institutes that teach peacebuilding, civic responsibility, and reconciliation—especially for youth and former combatants.

- Diaspora-Led Investment Forums
  Organize global forums where Nubian diaspora leaders can pledge support for schools, hospitals, and vocational centers in their ancestral lands.

- Youth Innovation Labs
  Create hubs where young people can learn coding, design, and entrepreneurship—turning creativity into community solutions.

Sustainability and Infrastructure

- Agricultural Cooperatives and Seed Banks
  Equip farmers with tools, drought-resistant seeds, and training in sustainable practices. Establish seed banks to ensure food security during crises.

- Renewable Energy Projects
  Introduce solar and wind energy solutions to power clinics, schools, and homes—reducing dependency on costly or inaccessible fuel sources.

- Reconstruction of Churches, Mosques, and Vital Infrastructure
  Rebuild places of worship destroyed by airstrikes—restoring spiritual sanctuaries for prayer, healing, and community resilience. Repair roads, water systems, and clinics to restore dignity and access to essential services.

Empowerment and Identity

- Women's Empowerment and Protection Programs
  Launch initiatives that protect women from violence, promote literacy, and support female entrepreneurship in crafts, agriculture, and trade.

- Cultural Preservation and Storytelling Archives
  Document Nuba traditions, languages, and testimonies through digital archives, books, and community museums to preserve identity and inspire pride.

Strategic Post-War Programs for Lasting Renewal

Once the guns fall silent, the real work begins. Post-war recovery must be guided not only by reconstruction, but by reconciliation, renewal, and reintegration. These programs aim to restore the soul of the Nuba Mountains and empower its people to flourish:

Transitional Justice and Truth Commissions

- Establish community-led truth commissions to document war crimes, displacement, and trauma.
- Promote restorative justice through public hearings, reparations, and memorialization.
- Ensure survivors' voices shape national healing and policy reform.

Civic Leadership and Governance Training

- Train local leaders in transparent governance, human rights, and participatory democracy.
- Support youth councils and women's leadership forums to foster inclusive decision-making.
- Build capacity for local administration/anti-corruption mechanisms.

Mental Health and Psychosocial Support Networks

- Expand trauma-informed counseling services across schools, churches, and clinics.
- Train community caregivers in grief support, resilience-building, and suicide prevention.
- Normalize mental health care as part of holistic healing.

Economic Recovery and Vocational Training

- Launch vocational centers offering training in carpentry, tailoring, mechanics, and digital skills.
- Provide microgrants and mentorship for small businesses and cooperatives.
- Create job placement programs for ex-combatants and displaced youth.

Interfaith Dialogue and Reconciliation Forums

- Convene regular gatherings of Christian, Muslim, and traditional leaders to foster mutual respect.
- Promote joint community service projects and shared worship events.
- Use scripture and storytelling to heal divisions and affirm shared humanity.

Curriculum Reform and Historical Inclusion

- Revise national curricula to include Nuba history, languages, and contributions.
- Develop peace education modules rooted in local wisdom and global ethics.
- Encourage academic research on Nuba resilience and cultural heritage.

Environmental Restoration and Land Rights

- Launch reforestation and soil restoration campaigns to heal war-damaged ecosystems.
- Secure land rights for displaced families and returning communities.
- Promote sustainable land use through community mapping and legal advocacy.

A Monument of Memory and Mercy
Where Grief Becomes Grace, and Silence Becomes Song

Let us not rebuild without remembrance. We propose the creation of a National Monument for the Martyred of the Nuba Mountains—a sacred space where names are etched, prayers are offered, and silence speaks louder than war.

This monument is more than stone—it is sacrament. It stands not only to remember the martyred, but to redeem their memory into mercy. Each name etched is a prayer. Each prayer whispered is a promise. Here, the wounds of war are not hidden—they are hallowed.

This monument shall honor civilians, clergy, children, and elders who were killed in the conflict. It will serve as a place of pilgrimage, education, and interfaith reflection. Designed by local artists and spiritual leaders, it will embody the resilience of the Nuba soul and the promise of peace.

Let this monument be a living covenant: that we will never again allow the Nuba to suffer in silence. Let it be a testimony that their lives were not lost in vain, and that memory shall guide mercy.

A Covenant of Hope
Faith in Action, Memory in Motion

Let this chapter be more than a record of suffering—it must become a covenant of hope. Hope is not passive—it is prophetic. This covenant is not written in ink alone, but in the lives we uplift, the systems we reform, and the communities we restore.

May the world stand with Nuba not only in prayer, but in partnership. May every developmental step echo the heartbeat of God, who remembers the forgotten and lifts the lowly.

This is a covenant between heaven and earth, between memory and mission. To stand with Nuba is to believe that healing is possible, that justice can be born from suffering, and that unity can rise from the rubble of division.

Together, we can turn the silence of neglect into a symphony of restoration.

Let Nuba rise—not as a footnote of history, but as a beacon of what unity in diversity can achieve.

May this covenant be

sealed with action,

sustained by faith, and

remembered as a turning point toward justice.

About the Author

Archbishop Dr. Paul Benjamin Yugusuk (Pa wolo) is a prophetic voice and servant leader in the Episcopal Church of South Sudan. As Archbishop of Central Equatoria Internal Province, he has walked with communities through war, displacement, and spiritual renewal—bringing comfort, courage, and advocacy to the margins of suffering.

His mission to the Nuba Mountains—undertaken amid bombardment and humanitarian crisis—became a living testimony of God's love among a people under siege. From scorched villages to hidden caves, Archbishop Pawolo bore witness to the cries of the oppressed and the hand of divine protection.

This book is the fruit of that mission: a sacred account of suffering and resilience, of mercy rippling through the shadows.

It breaks the silence of decades, revealing the spiritual endurance of the Nuba people and the hope that springs from faith in a God who liberates.

Archbishop Pawolo continues to lead with humility and boldness, advocating for justice, peace, and dignity across South Sudan and beyond. His life and ministry call readers to journey in prayer, compassion, and solidarity—until liberation is complete and faith shines with unshakable light.

www.ingramcontent.com/pod-product-compliance
Lightning Source LLC
LaVergne TN
LVHW052338100826
845147LV00020B/1107

* 9 7 8 0 9 9 1 3 5 3 3 5 4 *